ETERNITY IN A GRAIN OF SAND

By

Dean Gardner

Cover Painting By Aleksandre Vashakmadze

Leavitt Peak Press

ISBN: 978-1-967361-70-0 (sc)
ISBN: 978-1-967361-71-7 (e)

Rev. date: 05/30/2025

Contents

CHAPTER 1: open spaces in time

As the celestial
clocks configure
fate, the will to be
fights for a rightful
destiny through
the workings of
the biological clock.

There is the war
of principalities to
battle and existential
threats to conquer
when times and a half
throw being in time
onto the other side
of what matters.

It is the fury
of twisted rhetoric
that confounds
times when

mind struggles
through the debris
of being in nothingness.

Although the celestial
clocks tamper with the will
to be, being toward
Truth rebukes the wind
of darkness, and turns
to the light of vertical
column of time.

Then, the old man
meditates his way
to beauty, Truth
and love, as he feels
the deep touch
of The Spirit of Truth.

As he sits beneath
a white oak tree
in the garden of
The Hard Rock Café
he strums his guitar
and the scarlet rose
sings the anthem
of hope.

Radio Free America
carries the tune
across the globe

and the world
dances in the streets.

It is the death
of double speak
and the resurrection
of language that
brings joy, and
Lady Liberty
signs the liberation
of of mankind
from despotism.

*

While listening
to the wind
the old man
looked to the sky
searching for a way
out of the decadence
of corrupt regimes.

Turmoil struck
the lands with
twisted rhetoric
confounding
the times.

There was the acute
absence of Truth

but the old man
remained faithful
to The Unknown God.

Although the weight
of mindlessness
sunk hopes and
dreams into despair
the rhythm of
the universe spoke
of freedom.

How hearts longed
for life, liberty
and the pursuit
of happiness.

As the drums
of eternity stirred
his heart, he composed
a song of beauty
Truth, and love.

It was an anthem
of hope for a people
buried by
tyrannical regimes.

The scarlet rose
inspired by the piece
sang Truth to power

and the world listened
thirsting for deliverance.

Her voice echoed
across the streets
of brutalized cities
and valleys rose
with the promise
of Truth restored.

Although darkness covered
the globe with despair
and oppression smothered
the people, their song
brought the presence
of a light, a way through
the morass of times
and a half.

*

Journeying into
the unknown
and grounded in
the actual
peppermint birdie
undressed reality
while connecting to
the authentic article.

Upon seeing the workings

of what matters, she
moved mountains
of thought into
the substance of what
was there.

Then, stardust shone
upon the way, the Truth
and the life, as
the center of things
in themselves wrote
Truth upon her heart.

Then, the crystal
crow appeared through
the looking glass
of being in time
as her inner eye
penetrated one
dimensional existence.

Feeling the wind
pass through her
mind, she saw
endless possibility
upon a distant
horizon.

It was the climax
of the war between
the actual verses realities

as twisted rhetoric
climbed through being there.

It was the war
against double speak
that she faced
as The Unknown God
redeemed time.

Awakened by Truth
peppermint birdie
reached into the deep
touch as The Spirit
of Truth led her
beyond the immediate.

Then, Canis Lupis
embraced her
with the mysteries
of life, and she danced
across what was
there with beauty
Truth, and love.

*

Standing in the rain
feeling the warm drizzle
seeing a blue patch
in the cloudy sky
Annabel Lee tasted

the breath behind
what matters.

There was a trace
to hope that transcended
being there, as she left
being in nothingness
for being toward Truth.

To live with the way
the Truth, and the life
carried her far behind
her imagination
as beauty, Truth
and love wrote
the doctrine of being
toward Truth.

How awesome to be
in the land of the free
and brave.

Although shadows
spoke with double
speak, the language
bearing the authentic
article persevered.

It was that twisted
rhetoric confounded
the mindscape.

It was pure
music that liberated
her will to be.

The deep touch
of freedom formed
kisses of Truth.

Unearthing hidden meaning
from the debris of being
in nothingness, Annabel
Lee felt the rhythm
of the universe carry
her to the peace beyond
understanding through
the power of the way
the Truth, and the life.

It was her faith
in The Unknown
God that pulled
her into a rhapsody
of blue.

So, for a while
the rain stopped
and a warm
gentle breeze
comforted her.

*

Awakening to the light
of the way, the Truth
and the light, Annabel
Lee surfaced upon
the beyond, as her
thoughts triggered
the probe
into the unknown.

As she opened herself
to the authentic article
of being toward Truth
the drums of eternity
pounded what matters
into the experiential.

It was the beginning
of a living moment
that eclipsed being
in nothingness, as
pure music carried
her into as epiphany
of life, liberty and
the pursuit
of happiness.

Although the madness
of the world abounded
in her past, her mind,
pulled her onto an
even plane beyond

the reaches
of double speak.

She found Truth
through her faith
in The Unknown God.

It was the deep
touch from The Spirit
of Truth that filled
her with the anthem
of hope.

It was the light
of one-dimensional
existence that healed
her wounds.

Then, times and
a half passed, as
she unearthed hidden
meaning from the debris
of double speak.

Looking through a portal
in a parabola of time
she built her life as
a witness to the glory of
The Unknown God.

Waiting for Eagle
Hawk to return

from the war in
Vietnam, she listened
to the anthem
of hope, and her heart
followed the rhythm
of the universe.

*

It was the unleashing
of her will to be
that Annabel Lee
broke the grip
of twisted rhetoric
as she sunk tyrants
in the debris
of the no longer.

Advancing the domain
held by the authentic
article she struck
the will to power
with the awesome
strength of Truth
to power.

Although double speak
had filled the air
with abominations
she silenced being
in nothingness

with her belief
in the way, the Truth
and the life.

Then, pure music
brought life
to liberty across
the globe.

There had been
a hunger for
Truth while twisted
rhetoric dominated
the landscape
for times and a half.

Hearing the call
to life, liberty
and the pursuit
of happiness
Annabel Lee struck
the tyrants with
The Spirit of Truth
clearing the mindscape
with the way, the Truth
and the life.

So, the world danced
to the rhythm
of the universe, as
the drums of eternity

rolled freedom into
the heart of humanity.

How vital was
faith in The Unknown
God in launching
beauty, Truth, and
love across horizon
to horizon from
the beyond.

*

So, the front line
of the war of
principalities was the fight
against double speak
and the old man
was determined to
wipe out twisted rhetoric.

As he meditated
upon beauty, Truth
and love, a vast sea
of possibility opened
his mind to the way
the Truth, and the life.

Gathering the elements
of what matters, he
molded the living moment

into pure music.

Then, the rhythm
of the universe
precipitated the immediate
into one-dimensional
existence, and The Spirit
of Truth pyramided
power and might into
his thought.

How reaching into
the beyond brings
the way, the Truth
and the life into
the old man's muscle.

 It was reading Truth
from being in time
that led the old
man to faith
in The Unknown God.

So, he was prepared
to slay double speak
with his will to be.

Focused upon the actual
he built a fortress
of what truly matters.

He found his purpose

in serving The Unknown
God, and standing for life
liberty, and the pursuit
of happiness.

At his side was Olivia
from oblivion, an extra
terrestrial, and she
helped him orchestrate
an army of believers
in God almighty.

Together, they were
determined to wipe out
double speak with
the mysteries of life.

*

Within a stand
of trees, where
the shade of eternity
summons Truth
the old man feels
a forest of wonder
as the immediate
tickles thought
into endless
possibility.

Although the madness

in the world
flexes its muscles
he lives with
the peace beyond
understanding
through the way
the Truth, and the life.

As the anthem
of hope echoes
in his skull
he envisions beauty
Truth, and love.

It is an awakening
to what matters.

It is pure music
painted upon his
will to be.

Then, he looks
to the crystal
crow opening
the clouds
and he feels
the surge of
an epiphany.

As he basks
in the light

of forevermore
Olivia from oblivion
reaches into his
heart with the deep
touch.

There is the awesome
beauty from The Spirit
of Truth that
encompasses the living
moment.

How the old
man sees eternity
in a stand of trees.

Looking through a looking
glass of times and
a half, he sees the dance
of what matters.

Then, he bends a knee
worshiping
The Unknown God.

*

Following the way
the Truth, and the life
across the terrain
where rolling ridges
of death immerged

in times and a half
peppermint birdie
set out to see
the debris left
by double speak.

It was a vast wasteland.

As she came upon
the remains of a village
where life was
no longer there the wind
carried the smell
of rotting flesh.

How grief took
her to an open
grave where bodies
lay lifeless.

Looking beyond the moment
peppermint birdie
took an oath
to battle those
entrenched in double speak.

It was the language
of tyranny that
silenced the landscape.

Then, she heard a voice
coming from afar

singing a beautifully
sad song.

It was a child hiding
in the debris.

As peppermint birdie
approached the voice's
source, she met with
a little girl worn by terror.

Her name was Alice.

They talked for a while
and peppermint birdie
gained the little girl's trust.

Then, together
they left that village
and they left
the rolling ridges
of death.

*

While in meditation
beneath a white oak tree
in the garden
of The Hard Rock Café
the old man beheld
a disturbing image
that throttled his mind.

It was a vision
that depicted
the antichrist
through the workings
of artificial intelligence.

Through social media
the image captivated
humanity, signaling
the enslavement
of Western Civilization.

How the children
of God became
persecuted because
they saw through
artificial intelligence's
depiction of The Second
Coming.

It was the simulation
of the way, the Truth
and the life by
virtual reality.

From cunning minds
the antichrist ruled
the world with ruthless
power.

So, it became

a new form
of the war
of principalities.

Because some hungered
ever so sincerely
for the return
of Jesus Christ
they became deceived
by the antichrist
a creation of desperate
minds.

Although a remnant
of true believers remained
they were slaughtered
by the followers
of the antichrist.

How a reign
of terror forced
the remnant
to hide in shadows
while the army
of the antichrist
sought to crucify them.

Children of God beware.

*

To end double speak

and its wicked ways
Canis Lupis enlisted
in the army.

He wanted to fight
for freedom and he
wanted to help spread
the peace beyond
understanding.

As a young man
Canis Lupis committed
himself to the way
the Truth, and the life
and he lived with pure
music in his heart.

Learning from the old
man, Canis Lupis took
himself to worshiping
The Unknown God.

There was no doubt
in his mind
as he thought
himself through
a portal in a two
dimensional existence
onto the light of a vertical
column of time.

Reaching into splendor
he knew The Spirit
of Truth as the keeper
of what matters.

Although the world
abounded with madness
he guarded his faith
in The Unknown God.

It was his love
for life, liberty
and the pursuit
of happiness
that he became
dedicated to
the doctrine
of Lady Liberty.

He learned the power
of his faith when
he faced battle in
the war of principalities.

So, even in
fighting against
tyranny
he was relentless
in leading the charge
against twisted rhetoric.

Even when wounded
he held his stand.

*

As Lady Liberty
peppermint birdie
took the mantle
of power, she swiftly
asserted the strength
of the land of
the free and the brave.

Tyrants trembled before her.

Returning world peace
with the strong hand
of an awesome force
she brought an end
to the hatred that crippled
the Mid-East.

She quieted the storm
of war in Europe
and halted advance
of communism
in the Far-East.

Domestically, Lady
Liberty returned
manufacturing
to the shores

of stars and stripes.

Inflation was under control.

It became a country
of meritocracy
where each individual
could fulfill
the American dream
by hard work.

Shortly after the third
year of her presidency
an evil got to her
while she attended
a championship game.

There was a sniper
from above that gunned
her done.

One shot to her
forehead
and she was dead.

Canis Lupis was at her side.

It was a shock that
shook the world.

Although peppermint
birdie was dead

Lady Liberty lived on.

*

To hear the call
of Truth to power
how the heart pounds
with delight, as mind
conquers double speak
with the wat, the Truth
and the life.

Although the madness
of the world rages
in debilitating silence
the scarlet rose sings
with beauty, Truth and
life, as the sky opens on
wings of eternity.

So, her voices pours
pure music across
mountains and valleys
burying twisted rhetoric
forevermore.

As her anthem
of hope unearths
the will to be
from the debris
left by despots

the artist configures
the landscape of
the always already there.

Imaging beauty
Truth, and love, he
reveals a portal
in a parabola
of time where splendor
rises from space in time.

Then, intertwining her voice
with his will to be
they meditate into
the beyond with power
and strength.

Then, they rejoice
in the presence of
The Unknown God.

Leaving behind the noise
from emerging double
speak, they march
together with the children
of God to denizens of evil
and kill twisted rhetoric
at its source.

Obliterating denizens
of darkness, the light

of a vertical column
of time shines through
the folly of the will
to power with the grace
of The Spirit of Truth.

*

Reading the mysteries
of life inscribed
on the always already
there, the artist felt
the splendor of pure music
as he walked into
the everlasting.

Then, he sketched
what was there
with blood
and sweat, and a portal
to the beyond opened
his mind to eternity.

With thoughts on
the wings of forevermore
he uncovered hidden
meaning and the rhythm
of the universe filled
the chambers of his
heart with love.

It was an epiphany
of life, liberty
and the pursuit
of happiness, as
the scarlet rose
waved the banner
of the free and brave.

As The Unknown God
took them to what
matters they followed
the way, the Truth and
the life into the light
of a vertical column
of time and The Spirit
of Truth buried double
speak.

So, the will to power
fell into pits of pain.

So, twisted rhetoric
joined the no longer.

Returning to the here
in now, the artist looked
to shadows that concealed
tyrants and despots.

Then, he erased them.

It was the actuality

of Truth that purged
time present of what
was on the tongues
of evil.

*

To see the other
side where a parabola
of time defines
the moment, and pure
music fills the heart
with wondrous
sensations, the scarlet
rose breathes life
into being in time.

Following her into
the unknown
the artist mounted
his steed of iron
and thunder with
colors of being toward
Truth taking his inner
eye wherever the road
led.

It was freedom
articulating what
matters into his life
as he rode through

shadows of thought
and his heart felt
the glory of The Unknown
God on the other side.

Stopping at the edge
of space in time
he heard a star
spangled banner
liberate his mind.

Then, a cloud hid the sun.

Then, the rain beat hard.

Then, his dream
painted the wandering
of life through fields
of clover with
the scarlet rose
fulfilling his want
with the deep touch.

It was the scent
of the mysteries of life
that surrounded him
as he rode into eternity
on his cold steel
and hot muscle.

Then, the scarlet
rose sang the anthem

of hope, and his mind
surfaced in endless
possibility.

How being in concert
with beauty, Truth
and love brought
him closer to the way
the Truth, and the life.

*

So, the old man
meditated upon
the encompassing
onto the way, the Truth
and the life, and a one
dimensional existence
poured pure music into
the heart of endless
possibility.

To witness the grandeur
of The Unknown God
how an awakening
to The Spirit of Truth
brought the old man
into what matters.

As the day reached
into his visions

with the deep touch
he felt the earth
of being toward Truth
and it was good.

Although he felt
twisted rhetoric
try to wield the sword
of double speak
the old man struck down
the demonic inclusion
of the madness of the world.

Living in the actual
allowed him to see
through his inner eye
liberating times
and a half from
intruding thoughts.

Then, his vision
revealed the vastness
of endless possibility
as the energy of cosmic
consciousness was released
into being toward Truth.

As Olivia from oblivion
appeared in the clouds
he dreamed his way
onto her deep touch.

How her love for him
transcended all realities.

How his devotion to her
rose into the beyond.

So, the old man
conquered
twisted rhetoric
by feeling his way
into love everlasting.

*

Caught in a web
of nothingness
where pain crippled
thought, Eagle Hawk
plunged into darkness.

Drowning in an abyss
that tormented him
with memories
of his tours of duty
his heart bled
with an ache
of cruel thoughts.

He felt abandoned
in his suffering.

Wave after wave

of dread took him
to the brink
of the no longer.

He felt better off dead.

Walking down back
roads, he saw
an old man sitting
beneath a white
oak tree.

He said that he
saw Eagle Hawk
from far away.

Although Eagle Hawk
did not feel like
a conversation
he listened to
the old man.

There was something
special about
the sound of his voice.

He told Eagle Hawk
that the road he
was on was not
a dead end, but
the beginning of a journey
into endless possibility.

Pointing to the horizon
the old man told
him that beyond
there was the domain
of the crystal crow.

And he said
that the crystal
crow was surrounded
by the anthem of hope.

Eagle Hawk was touched
with wonder.

From then on
they were friends.

*

It was that the will
to power spawned
the integrated collective
as an army of warriors
directed to crush
being toward Truth
and its progeny.

It was Lady Liberty
that led the will
to be onto life
liberty, and
the pursuit

of happiness.

Consequently, the war
of principalities involved
the clashing of these
two forces –
the integrated collective
and the children of God.

As battle after
battle raged in
the streets, the life
of freedom approached
the no longer.

Then, Lady Liberty
as a symbol
of what matters
leaned on her meditation
for the means to victory.

So, she gathered
the will to be
as the root
of being in time
and raised the banner
of Truth.

From far and wide
they came
across the land

village and town
and city, pledging
allegiance to the life
of freedom.

They were called
freedom fighters
and they rid the land
bearing twisted rhetoric.

The will to power
collapsed, and double
speak was slain
by Truth to power.

So, the world experienced
times of peace and prosperity
although lurking, generations
of the will to power grew in shadows.

CHAPTER 2: the backroads of mind

Suddenly, the earth
of the will to power
heaved chaos
into the front
of what was there
and the world spun
into a wasteland
of despair.

As the rubble
from the collapse
of humanity
cluttered times
and a half
darkness filled
hearts with the cold
chill of existential
dread.

It was that the blood
of Truth emptied

into silence
until the muscle
of pure music
emancipated hope
as the children of God
rose against the tirade
of twisted rhetoric
the language of tyranny.

Then, the fight for
freedom griped the doctrine
of the landscape.

Then, the war
of principalities
ripped minds
from a deep
sleep, and Lady
Liberty gathered
a remnant of those
who sought Truth.

Marching into bastions
of decadence
they pounded the drums
of eternity that shattered
the will to power
and freedom rose
across the world.

Returning to life, liberty

and the pursuit
of happiness, the land
of the free and brave
stifled the control
of despots who tormented
the people with deception.

Once again, the anthem
of hope was the language
celebrating with beauty
Truth, and love.

*

Wading through the debris
 of twisted rhetoric
that crushed the mind
that wounded the heart
with daggers of language
that corrupted thought
bled from the living self
the will to be raised
the banner representing
beauty, Truth, and love.

Out from the darkness
where the will to power
dominated the doctrine
of the landscape, came
the complete control
of humanity, where life

liberty, and the pursuit
of happiness died.

It was the objective
of the tyrants
to dominate minds
with the desire
to control the thinking
of the populace
through depraved media.

So, the people
could not trust
weaponized media
or government
the puppets of tyrants.

With Lady Liberty
as the figure head
of peppermint birdie
staged an assault
on the wall of deception
and Canis Lupis stood
at her side, as they
followed the way
the Truth, and the life.

Filled with The Spirit
of Truth, they gathered
the children of God
into a formidable

force with the purpose
of returning trust in the land.

Feeding Truth to power
they sang the anthem
of hope, and minds
read the love
of The Unknown God
in their heart.

The people saw
that life, liberty
and the pursuit
of happiness had
been stifled, and they
breathed victory over
those who flaunted
their twisted rhetoric.

*

Shattering the constraints
of being there, being toward
Truth built a monument from
meditation, and what was there
signaled the presence of the actual.

Caressing the moment
with passion peppermint
birdie thrust breath
into the life of belief

as she danced in the light
of one dimensional
existence to the delight
of Canis Lupis.

They were entwined
with the vision that
revealed life, liberty
and the pursuit
of happiness
from the beyond.

They fed on manna
from heaven, as they
released the language
that maintained
the doctrine
of the landscape.

It was the architecture
founded upon the actual.

Then, they followed
the language of beauty
Truth, and love
with the anthem of hope
and tines changed
into splendor.

Then, their minds
were filled with

thoughts lit by
stardust, and they
knew true love
from The Unknown God.

As being there
scrambles beneath
rocks in fear
of The Unknown God
times and a half
ignite with love
but being there does
not understand
how it can be loved.

So, the will to power collapses.

So, the will to be
actualizes with life
liberty, and the pursuit
of happiness into being
toward Truth.

*

As the self works
its way through
the world through
the madness
of the world
through dark hearts

that lead
a country into chaos
freedom seems so very
far away and the chains
of oppression bind
minds for times
and a half until self
dies in despair.

Although death is
relief from being there
a welcomed friend
while pain digs deep
into the heart, a remnant
rises with the desire
for life, liberty
and the pursuit
of happiness.

Then, the silence
of slavery is
answered by pure
music from beyond.

Then, the anthem of hope
rings through the streets
where ready bodies gather
to restore freedom.

With the muscle
of their belief

in the peace beyond
understanding through
the way, the Truth
and the life, they march
against the will to power
as the will to be liberates
itself with weapons
of beauty, Truth, and love.

It is that the want
for freedom opens
minds to endless
possibility, and trumpets
announce the presence
of Lady Liberty.

The purpose of the revolt
is to restore life
to a people who only want
to live and let live.

*

As the passion
for pure music moves
mountains into mind
appearance dissolves
in mystic clouds
and the anthem of hope
marches into the center
of the will to be.

Eclipsing time and times
and a half, being toward
Truth plants the idea
of the beyond into mind
as thought reveals
the mystery of life, the love
of The Unknown God.

A message is sent
from The Spirit of Truth that
announces the redemption
of time, delivering
the peace beyond
understanding through
the way, the Truth
and the life.

Driven from the absence
dwelling in being
in nothingness, self
hears the call of first
principles that leads to
the death of twisted
rhetoric.

Having been fed
double speak
from the cradle to the grave
self falls into the hands
of the will to power.

It is the end
of the will to be
that smothers the breath
of life, as bodies
stagger heartless, mindless
onto day after day.

Crippled by demons
using twisted rhetoric
as the control of the will
to power, self longs for
the return of the passion
for pure music.

Through the looking
glass of being in time
the inner eye
is given to the children
of God to follow
the way to The
Unknown God.

Then, life is
restored to heart
as mind
thinks its way
to beauty, Truth
and love.

*

In the wilds
where being there
writes beauty, Truth
and love into unmarked
graves, the will to be
struggles through
dark times
when twisted rhetoric
blocks the light
from the beyond
and trust
dies from despair.

It is the alienation
of the individual
from what matters
that rips the heart
into pieces of bloody
meat and the self
bleeds in solitude.

Laying waste hopes
and dreams held
by the individual destroys
purpose as the will
to be is thrown into misery.

As double speak
corrupts language
trust, once born
by media, drops dead.

It is time
that the children
of God take back
life from despots
drunk on the will
to power.

As the anthem
of hope rings
across lands
consumed by dread
being toward Truth
rises from ashes
and whispers in the wind
restore life, liberty and
the pursuit of happiness.

Then, the will
to be speaks
Truth to power
as the force
grounded in
the dignity of humanity
pounds Truth
into the living moment.

Then, Lady Liberty steps
on the neck of despots
and individual rights
live once again
in the close at hand.

*

A song floats
across mind
as thought follows
the will to be
actualizing
being in time
and heart yearns
for beauty, Truth
and love.

Although shadows
breaking through
silence enslave his
hopes and dreams
as twisted rhetoric
clogs his desires
with venomous
double speak
the old man
climbs into meditation
to witness the presence
of the way, the Truth
and the life.

It is in a war
of principalities
within his mind
that the old man
fights demons

that drive madness
into his mind
but he fights on.

.

Breaking through
bastions
caging thought
 controlling his heart
with tentacles twisted
across his throat
the blood of being
toward Truth triumphs
over the wicked schemes
of despots.

Although strangled
by indifference
the old man takes
to the freedom
belonging to the actual.

Then, he sees
Lady Liberty weeping
over bodies dead
in their faithlessness
in hollows
where their being in
nothingness suffers
in pain of disbelief.

Then, he sees

the children of God
with faith in
The Unknown God
rise into the light
of a vertical
column of time
consummating beauty
Truth and love
in each individual
with pure music.

*

As pure music
shuffles feet
to the rhythm
of the universe
with the actual
pounding the drums
of eternity
with beauty, Truth
and love, her body
moves into the light
of always already
there, and the moment
breathes epiphany
into times and a half.

Focusing her inner
eye upon far reaches
where mind mirrors

life, as trumpets
pyramid eternity
into the here
and now, Olivia
from oblivion arrives
in time present
and the old man
fastens his heart
to the sway of her body.

It is love.

It is the dance
of what matters.

Then, she takes
her will to be
onto the old man
and he owns
into her deep touch.

Through the window
opening endless
possibility to being
toward Truth, Olivia
from oblivion forms
the substance
of true love
grounded upon
her rock of faith
in the way, the Truth

and the life.

Then, the old man
trusts his heart.

Then, pure music
takes them
to horizons
beyond space
in time
where the air
eases life
into the living
moment and
they share
their wounds.

*

Leaving behind a world
of chaos that ripped
her heart from time
present, traveling through
the universe of being
in time, she took
to astro-projection
and she reached through
space in time
to the other side
of being in nothingness
where life supported

spiritual growth.

As she felt
the rhythm
of the universe pull
her into the center
of things in themselves
where star dust
defined the living
moment, she came
upon the brain waves
of an old man.

He sat beneath
a white oak tree
deep in meditation.

A melody of pure
music surrounded
him with the deep touch.

As she heard
the anthem of hope
sung by the crystal
crow, she placed
herself in the company
of the old man.

Across the sky
a message wrote
beauty, Truth

and love into her heart
bringing freedom
to her mind
untangling the tentacles
from her throat.

As the old man left
his trance
he saw the form
of splendor before him.

Then, they felt
a deep touch
of the mystery
of life, and space
in time married
their will to be
to belief
in The Unknown God.

So, they live on
in wonder
embraced by
The Spirit of Truth.

*

As the sky fills
life with dreams
of a starry night
and the wind gusts

in twilight wonder
trumpets summon
the everlasting
into time present.

It is the call
of the wilds
that stirs the heart
with want
and his heart
feels the way
onto forevermore.

Reaching into distant
stars, his mind
connects with the will
to be and times
and a half orbit
with the sound
of pure music.

Then, a cry
for the peace
beyond understanding
reaches onto beams
cast by the moon
and his blood
mixes with hopes.

Then, launching into a sunrise
when the mystical mixes

with earthy elements
the air triggered thoughts
and mind scrambled
for the dawn.

Then, times change
as her voice covers
the ache in his heart.

Then, she touches him
with freedom
born from belief
in the way, the Truth
and the life.

As he pyramids
into being in time
pure music sways
through her form
and he feels
the epiphany
of the light
from one-dimensional
existence.

It is the actuality
of her passionate kiss
that drives him
into what matters.

*

Hooking her destiny
to a purple star
she sings pure music
into the air, followed
by the dance
onto forevermore
and the walls
of double speak tumble
down in ashes.

As an anthem of hope
cascades from the sky
as the first light
known to the dawn
creases the heavens
with sweet dreams
she takes to the deep
touch, and the artist
configures space in time
into thunder and fire.

Then, the presence
of the scarlet rose
showers his times
with pure music
and the rhythm
of the universe
leads him ever
closer to the way
the Truth, and the life.

It is the message
from The Spirit of Truth
that lights his mind
with splendor.

The actuality of the will
to be conquers the will
to power, issuing
an epiphany of beauty
Truth, and love
as the scarlet rose
kisses him with star dust.

Then, a star spangled
dream eases through
his mind, releases his
heart from the constraints
of twisted rhetoric
and his want for blessings
from The Unknown
God surfaces in his soul.

Leaping out of himself
the artist constructs
the struggle of self
against the madness
festering in the world
and the scarlet rose
delights him with
her presence.

Bringing life, liberty
and the pursuit
of happiness to his
will to be, she kisses
him with treasures
of being toward Truth.

Thankful, he praises
The Unknown God
for the gift of her love.

*

As a dream replaces
what is there
when infinity ends
when the rhythm
of the universe collapses
space in time, pure
music from the everlasting
endures onto eternity
something that has no
beginning and no end.

As being in time
lives in the always
already there
the will to be
mirrors the drift
of all and everything.

It is that infinity
 births the agenda
of the empiricist
to manipulate
the self and corrupt
the heart and mind.

Then, being toward
Truth speaks Truth
to power.

Then, the inner
eye sees beauty
Truth and love
in The Unknown God.

For the empiricist
the origin of space
in time grounds
itself in hypotheses
while being in time
reflects the always
already there.

 While self triggers
the want for what
matters, being there
twists thought with
double speak
and humanity falls to
the hands of despots.

Then, Truth is wiped out.

Then life falls
into a merciless pit.

So, the will to be
struggles under
the weight of being
in nothingness.

Although a remnant
is mutilated, self
endures to rise again.

*

As pure music
penetrates the darkness
with the light
from beyond
dancing into hearts
pronouncing beauty
Truth, and love
into the living moment
infusing trust in the love
of The Unknown God
peppermint birdie
accepts the challenge
to lead the country
back to a power
house of freedom

for the world.

Then, the world took
notice to the prowess
of a nation founded
upon life, liberty
and the pursuit
of happiness.

Then, peppermint
birdie became known
as Lady Liberty.

So, the madness
of the world ceased.

As the anthem of hope
rang through the streets
across mountains to the seas
across meadows and valleys
onto all horizons
of space in time
a world united in the peace
beyond understanding.

As hearts opened
to the melody
of The spirit of Truth
as minds ended chaos
as Lady Liberty won
the trust of the world

twisted rhetoric hid
in shadows, as she
spoke Truth to power.

Carrying the world
into the light
of one-dimensional
existence, through
a portal in a parabola
of time, she established
prosperity to all lands
and ended double speak
in gatherings.

Then, the world
emerged
as a united people
free from the chains
of despotism.

*

Wedded to the way
the Truth, and the life
accepting The Spirit
of Truth Lady Liberty
brought an era of beauty
Truth, and love
and the world left
the rule of madness
accepting the love

of The Unknown God.

As she spoke
Truth to power
despots hid
in their darkness
while being toward
Truth pulled them
into a sea
of the no longer.

So, pure music
filled the air
with the anthem
of hope, and the drums
of eternity pounded
light into shadows
of doubt, as a nation
of promise confirmed its
faith in The Unknown God.

Then, the pursuit
of what matters
became the mission
of the world
erasing twisted rhetoric
from language
and the doctrine
of the landscape
became freedom of
living and letting live.

As minds probed
the unknown
as thought reflected
the always already
there, trusting in
the message of Truth
echoing in the heart
the people walked
in the light of epiphany.

Then, Lady Liberty
announced the end
of the wasteland
bringing the world
into lands
of hopes fulfilled.

*

So, double speak
corrupts the mind
and poisons the heart
as hard times ruin
the image of self
enslaving thoughts
with twisted rhetoric
until life descends into
being in nothingness.

To destroy the individual
and replace it with

the integrated collective
retards the will to be
until dependence on
despots turns the people
into cattle.

It is that the will
to power seeks
control over the human
spirit, erasing faith
through the depravity of
contextual materialism.

Then, hopes and dreams
are replaced by conformity
and political correctness.

So, Lady Liberty
lead the charge
against double speak
as Eagle Hawk
and Annabel Lee
conquered the will
to power with life
liberty, and the pursuit
of happiness.

To liberate self
from slavery under
despots, the muse
drives the artist

onto the restoration
of beauty, Truth
and love.

It is that The Spirit
of Truth pyramids
being toward Truth
with the strength
and courage to
dethrone the despots
who live by the will
to power.

So, hopes and dreams
and freedom flourish
in the life of the world
as trumpets awaken
self to epiphany.

*

As the old man
carved clouds
into the twilight
and the sky fell
into darkness
he astro
projected himself
into distant horizons
of time, leaving behind
the madness in the world

the chaos brought
by those possessed
with the will to power.

With The Spirit
of Truth filling him
with visions, Olivia
from oblivion showed
him the other side
of spaced in time
the source of the always
already there.

It was his drive
to see the way
the Truth, and the life
into the immediate
that they conquered
the fear of the unknown
as they joined
a harvest of souls.

As they slipped
through a portal
in a two-dimensional
existence, the actuality
of The Unknown God's
love took them
into the living moment
where the peace beyond
understanding reigned.

Then, he felt
the return of beauty
Truth, and love.

Then, pure music
eclipsed darkness.

It was that
they embraced
the calling
upon their heart
and twisted
rhetoric of despots
vanished in the wind
of the everlasting.

So, they lived lives
infused with meaning
with life, liberty, and
the pursuit of happiness.

*

Through the looking
glass of the crystal
crow, visions from the other
side of space in time
surface, and the light
of one-dimensional
existence emanates
beauty, Truth, and love.

To transcend
the trappings
of being in
nothingness
the artist listens
to pure music
from The Unknown God
as his muse embraces
him with passion.

In the wilds
of want, where
a forest grows
with the desire
to be a wilderness
being there rejects
the way, the Truth
and the life:
however, the will
to be purposes
the freedom
in the life, liberty
and the pursuit
of happiness.

Seeing the face
of evil, the artist
turns to the message
from The Spirit
of Truth.

Then, his being
toward Truth
purposes forevermore
into the living moment
and vertical
column of time
shines upon him.

Then, the muse
surrounds him
with epiphany
after epiphany.

There is thunder
in his blood.
There is hope
in his heart.

There is light
in his eyes.

Then, the artist
and his muse
soar into joy
and wonder.

*

As mysteries of life
feed curiosity with
wonder, as mind images
the other side of what

is there, as want to
fathom the unknown
breeds hunger
self rides the rhythm
of the universe to
gather an understanding
of what matters.

With the freedom
to probe things in
themselves, self travels
through space in time
as the inner eye
perceives the interstices
of the will to be.

It is that pure
music defines
the doctrine
of the landscape
although twisted
rhetoric poisons
thought in the world.

It is a war
of principalities
between being
toward Truth
and being there.

Where life, liberty

and the pursuit
of happiness matters
being toward Truth
prospers in the blood
of the living moment.

Where double speak
and twisted rhetoric
dominates the here
and now, thinking
vanishes, and the world
becomes more and more
a wasteland under
the control of despots.

So, the old man
meditates on the way
the Truth, and the life.

So, Lady Liberty
marches against
the madness
of the world.

Although being there
employs the will to power
to confound thought
and cripple minds
The Spirit of Truth
opens visions of beauty

Truth, and love.

*

Listening to pure music
cruising the land from sea
to shining sea, riding
the rhythm of the universe
in the light of what
matters, mind leaps
from darkness
filling time present
with the glory of
The Unknown God
and the way, the Truth
and the life opens eternity
onto the immediate.

As the voice
of forevermore
echoes across
space in time
as the heart
joins the drums
of eternity
the self mirrors
in the here and
now, what is
of the always
already there.

Then, the light
of a vertical
column of time
delivers the soul
to a house of
many mansions.

Gathering five
smooth stones
in defense of life
liberty, and the pursuit
of happiness, the artist
travels through a parabola
of time to victory over
double speak.

It is the anthem of hope
that multiplies his strength.

It is the beauty
Truth, and love
created by
The Spirit of Truth
that takes the artist
into a frontier
where dreams
of freedom flourish.

So, mind is freed
from doubt.

*

CHAPTER 3: connecting to the beyond

As the integrated
collective formed
an army directed
by the will to power
human rights disappeared
along with beauty, Truth
and love.

It was a time
after peppermint
birdie was assassinated
when being toward
Truth went underground.

Canis Lupis rose
as a leader
of those following
the way, the Truth
and the life.

Although they were

persecuted, the underground
was resourceful
in maintain the principles
of life, liberty, and the pursuit
of happiness.

Although the integrated
collective hunted them
down, the underground
persevered in shadows
as the resistance.

So, Eagle Hawk
became a general
in the resistance
and the old man
became an advisor.

The artist was held
in prison by those
of double speak
for being outspoken
for beauty, Truty, and life.

So, the hub
of the resistance
was Canis Lupis
the old man and Olivia
from oblivion, Eagle
Hawk and Annabel
Lee, and the artist's muse.

Together, they formed
the lead to the resistance
as they meditated
their way through
a connection to
The Spirit of Truth.

How powerful they
grew in their faith
in The Unknown God.

*

Gathering in the garden
of The Hard Rock Café
the hub of freedom fighters
outlined the plan for
the resistance.

During their meeting
the old man meditated
his way to the other
side of being in time
and he saw the way
the Truth, and the life
through a portal
in a two-dimensional
existence.

It was a penetration
into what matters

that clarified issues
of defense.

Sharing his vision
with Eagle Hawk
opened the inner
eye of the general
who believed in
peace through
strength.

Their current strategy
was speaking Truth
to power.

Throughout the world
the hub established
a network that maintained
the cause of life
liberty, and the pursuit
of happiness.

Through social media
the cause of freedom
carried a message
of hope.

Because the will
to power tried
to silence the sites
of the underground

their identity
left no trace.

They shifted location
and identity in order
not to be found.

Across the world
there were tens
of thousands
of Hard Rock Cafés
some visible and
some invisible.

Although freedom
fighters orchestrated
an anthem of hope
across the world
the will to power
confounded the world
with double speak.

It was a war of principalities.

*

As the living moment
eclipsed time and times
and a half, a portal
to the mysteries
of life filled the will
to be with the substance

of things in themselves \t
the building blocks
of what matters.

It was the grammar
of being in times
that spread
the doctrine of
the mindscape
as understanding
grew into the pure
music of always
already there.

How meditating
on the way, the Truth
and the life enlightened
being toward Truth
to beauty, Truth, and love.

Thus, the physics
of the old man
rose with the sunrise
onto the everlasting.

Reading the subtext
that was there
in reality, he
unearthed hidden
meaning, and he saw
the grandeur of actuality.

It was the spirituality
of the actual defined
the purpose
of the will to be, which
was buried by the debris
left by the madness
in the world.

It was that The Spirit
of Truth overcame
double speak with
beauty, Truth and
love through the grandeur
of the actual.

So, it is The Unknown
God that appears through
the actual while humanity is
buried in the realities
of being there.

So, it is that the actual is
the reflection of the divine.

So, the old man
conquers twisted
rhetoric through
his meditations.

*

To see the divine in

what is there
appearing through
a portal in a two
dimensional existence
a parabola of time
opens the inner eye
to Truth.

Although the madness
in the world obfuscated
access to what matters
by the number figuring
of twisted rhetoric
the old man
persevered with his
visions of the actual.

While shadows
of twisted rhetoric
concealed Truth
with its noise
the old man
did not fall
into confusion but
rose in understanding
what was there.

Then, the crystal
crow launched
a mindscape
with beauty, Truth

and love.

Then, a vertical
column of time
lit access to
the divine.

It was a shattering
of the barriers
set by double
speak that opened
his self to pure music.

So, the old man's
will to be unearthed
Truth from the rubble
of the madness
in the world.

As the crystal crow
orchestrated beauty
Truth and love, the old
man meditated beyond
being in nothingness
and heard the voice
of The Spirit of Truth.

*

Then, Olivia from oblivion
reached into the old
man's mind, reading

his brainwaves.

Then, she believed
her way into what
matters, coinciding
her thoughts with his.

Together, they rode
the rhythm
of the universe
into the light of one
dimensional existence.

As they approached
the center of things
in themselves
The Spirit of Truth
opened their inner
eye to the presence
of The Unknown God
in the divine.

Gathering visions
that eclipsed the here
and now, they gave
thanks to God almighty
for their understanding.

Then, they left
their meditation
returning to The Hard

Rock Café.

Sharing their vision
with Eagle Hawk
and Annabel Lee
they spread their
encounter with the divine.

So, their vision
liberated the world
from double speak
as the thunder
of always already
there awakened hearts
with pure music.

So, it was that
Lady Liberty charged
the world with
the anthem of hope.

As the scarlet rose
inspired the artist
to color the will
to be with pure music
the children of God
had the strength to wipe
out bastions
of double speak.

Although one battle

was won, it was not
the end of the war
of principalities.

*

Plunging ever deeper
into the unknown
Canis Lupis explored
endless possibility
with the passion
of intense want.

Uncovering hidden
meaning, he unearthed
the mysteries
of life buried in
time and times and half.

There was a two
dimensional existence
in his mind that colored
the sky blood red.

There was a trumpet
announcing the beginning
of what matters
as the other side
of a vast sea rose
covering mountains.

Then, Canis Lupis

saw life onto eternity
soar across
his mindscape.

It was the glory
of The Unknown God
that appeared before
him, as a one-dimensional
existence, and pure music
carried the living moment
upon wings of forevermore.

Although the encounter
exploded his mind
he felt the peace
beyond understanding.

Pulling out of trance
he felt a heated sweat
on his brow and
his hands were on fire.

So, he had touched the beyond.

So, he felt the awesome
presence of The Spirit of Truth.

Then, he wrote the anthem of hope.

*

As pure music carried

across the land
the anthem of hope
echoed in the skulls
of the free and brave.

It was an awakening
to what matters, as
trumpets heralded
the living moment

It was the divine
revealed through
the actual that
brought life to a land
that wandered.

Although Truth would
not be silenced, twisted
rhetoric fought against
it with poisoned speech.

As the war
of principalities
raged in darkness
the artist painted
the mystery born
from The Spirit of Truth.

So, the light
of the everlasting
issued the drums

of eternity leading
the charge into
bastions of double speak.

Following the rhythm
of the universe
the children of God
embraced the words
of the divine written
upon their hearts.

Then, the scarlet rose
brought loving kindness
to the here and now
as the deep touch
moved worlds into
the peace beyond
understanding.

Then, The Unknown God
redeemed time, bringing
beauty, Truth, and love
as a way of life.

*

Feeling the pain
of being trapped
in a quagmire
where the fumes
of being there

smother the living
moment, being toward
Truth fights for life
liberty, and the pursuit
of happiness.

So, the fortress
of twisted rhetoric
crumbled into dust
as pure music rose
from the death
of double speak
and being in time
found freedom.

It was that
the chains
of depravity
let go their hold
on the children
of God.

Although wounds
cut deep, victory
over being there
blossomed into
sheer joy.

It was time to dance
in the streets
celebrating faith

in The Unknown God.

It was the determination
of the underground
in the war of principalities
that triumphed over
the will to power.

Singing the anthem
of hope, the scarlet
rose saluted the stars
and stripes forever.

How Lady Liberty
rejoiced across
the other side
of what was there.

Then, the artist
painted a two
dimensional existence
with the blood of battle.

So, tyrants of a vile citadel
joined the no longer.

*

While the old man
meditated in the library
of The Hard Rock Café
he beheld the rhythm

of the universe carry
his thoughts to
the elements of life.

He saw that
the will to be
is the fundamental
core of life and was
present in all
forms of life
from weeds to flowers
to forests of trees
vast and wide, from
the worm to the ant to
tiger, ape and mankind.

So, at the core
of all forms of life
is the will to be.

It is the seminal energy of life.

As building blocks
it leads to consciousness
of being in time.

As the presence
of being in time
the actual presents
existence into
the physical world.

As existence reaches
into the actual
the mysteries of life
become evident
through the domain
of the divine.

At this point
being toward Truth
surfaces, along with
its adversary being there.

The disposition
of being there
is the will to power
while the constitution
of being toward Truth
is life, liberty and
the pursuit of happiness.

All this and more
the old man beheld
in the library of
The Hard Rock Café.

*

Stirring in times
and a half, denizens
of evil growl deception
into the here and now.

As the serpent
tongue of twisted
rhetoric corrupts
what matters
the old man gathers
The hub of Truth.

They tear down
the walls
of double speak
and slay the serpent
With Truth.

There is endless
possibility to
the mysteries
of life, while
nothingness
is the future
of hidden meaning.

The Truth bears
witness in
the light of
the present, while
twisted rhetoric exists
in shadows of absence

So, Olivia from oblivion
an extra-terrestrial
speaks Truth to power

although she fears
that she might not
have a soul.

She fears the unknown
while the old man
ventures through
the unknown to
gather meaning from
endless possibility.

It is an adventure
to explore
the unknown, to
understand the workings
of the divine.

How the actual precedes
and eclipses reality.

Reality comes from
personal experience
and is in as many
forms as there
are individuals.

There is only Truth
to the actual
and is drawn from
The beyond.

*

Although times and
a half enshroud
the self with gloom
and dread, the will to be
endures with the passion
of purpose led by hope.

As pure music fills
the heart with beauty
Truth and love, Olivia
from oblivion reaches
the deep touch
of what matters,

It is that she
Is from a far
away presence
in a godless
world.

Through her connection
to the old man
she learns
of the way, the Truth
and the life, but
her mind, at times
entertains doubt.

Although she wonders
if the old man's faith
is folly, she sees how

his faith strengthens
him, giving him
the courage to explore
the unknown, and live
on the edge.

As he meditates through
corridors of thought
he search for Truth
and the anatomy
of being in time.

As they ride
the rhythm
of the universe
together, she feels
the presence
of The Unknown God
the actuality
of pure music
as an energy
from a vertical
column of time.

It is that the will
to be manifests itself
through pure music
as The Spirit
of Truth opens
her inner eye
to the veritable

the actuality
of the divine.

*

When linear time
leaps into a vertical
column of time, cosmic
consciousness pours
pure music into
the immediate, and
the heart of things
in themselves dances
onto forevermore.

As self perceives
the divine
in actuality
the limitations
of linear space and
time drops away
as eternity opens
the inner eye
to what matters.

So, peppermint birdie
received the kiss
of cosmic consciousness.

It was the deep
touch of vertical

column of time
that she felt, as she
meditated upon
The Spirit of Truth.

Then, thunder in her
veins took her
onto a one
dimensional existence
as she explored
the unknown.

On the other side
of being in nothingness
she saw a house
of many mansions
and the anthem
of hope rose in praises
to The Unknown God.

How precious her
vision of the actual
as her meditation
gave her the splendor
of the divine.

Returning to the here
in now, peppermint
birdie listened to the wind
and the mysteries
of life wrote across

her mind with beauty
Truth, and love.

Then, the crystal
crow delivered her
to the strength of being
toward Truth.

*

While the light
of the moon
replaces the white
of the chrysanthemums
with the pale
of what is there
the artist maps
the constitution
of being in time
as the actual
replaces reality.

There is up
and there is down.

There is left
and there is right.

There n is the authentic
article in the presence
of opposites.

There is right
and there is wrong.

There is good
and there is bad.

Opposites exist
in a quadrant scale
as extremes.

Little is all bad
or all good.

Little is all right
or all wrong.

So, the artist defines
his painting
in figure and ground.

Then, he travels
to the other
side of being there
finding being toward
Truth, and a parabola
of time appears in
the close at hand.

As the image
of his intent
grows into a mystery
of life, the scarlet

rose leads him onto
the authentic article.

Then, he hears
pure music cover
times and a half
with the colors
of epiphany
and he illustrates
the journey
into the beyond.

So, the scarlet rose
becomes the figure
being thrown
into the ground
of the always
already there.

*

How the moon
lit the darkness
with mysteries
of life, as splendor
radiated with Truth
across a river of hope.

It was at the edge
of the river that
linear time painted

a two-dimensional
existence with the aroma
of forevermore, and life
embraced the moon.

How the divine
spoke to the heart
as the river
seized the moment.

Then, memories
of the little brown
duck came up
from the bottom
of the lake
with a smile.

So, the artist
drew the breath
of freedom
beneath a full
moon, and muted
colors spoke Truth
to power.

It was the detail
flowing into
times and a half
that defined things
in themselves, and
the artist painted

waves of thought.

Then, the muse
carried his mind
far beyond the here
in now with beauty
Truth, and love.

There was a song
in the wind
that reached
into his will
to be with
the symmetry
of the divine.

How the anthem
of hope flourished
in his bones.

Moving from what
was to what shall
be, the artist
painted a portal
in a parabola
or time lit
by the light
of moon beams.

*

Then, a river

of blood flowed
through the streets
where life ended
and twisted rhetoric
lit a fire across
the swift current.

Although lives lost
were buried in mass
graves, they rose
in the hearts
of countrymen.

It was corrupt minds
that fed on the will
to power, devouring
the hopes of a nation.

It was
the underground
destined to restore
the land of the free
and brave that battled
against tyranny.

As the war blasted
the age, Eagle Hawk
marched against
that will to
power and erased
twisted rhetoric.

How the corrupt
churned in open
graves, their destiny
of decay.

How the river
of blood spoke
of the lives that
died in the fight
against double speak.

Meditating at the edge
of the river of blood
the old man wept
over the loss of so many.

Then, he saw them rise
into the sky
of forevermore.

Following them
with his inner eye
to a safe haven
in the sky
he heard a chorus
sing the anthem
of hope.

It was pure
music as
a testament to

The Unknown God.

*

As the crystal crow
spread its wings
eternity lit the moment
with wonder and splendor
and pure music pyramided
a bond of trust
within being in time.

There was the embrace
of Truth that carried
the substance of life
into the here and now
restoring belief
in The Unknown God

Then, the crystal crow
flew into a parabola
of time, and a portal
to one-dimensional
existence appeared
on the other side
of the will to be.

Then, a multitude
of colors rained
down, as star
dust, and forevermore

danced in the mind.

Although being in time
comes to an end, the will
to be carries on
to the everlasting.

How the mysteries
of life are concealed
in layers of reality
while the actual
of what is there
in the close at hand
points to the divine.

So, reality buries
the substance
of what is there
in hidden meaning.

So, the actual speaks
life into the living moment
as The Spirit of Truth
reveals beauty
truth and love.

How the unknown
yields to the will
to be, as being in time
grows in the light
of cosmic

consciousness.

Then, the crystal crow
fills the mind
with images of awe
and being toward
Truth explores
what is there, finding
what matters.

*

Advancing through
a corridor of time
to the beginning'
of the infinite
the artist found
himself in a forest
of thought.

Then, he saw
how eternity was
founded upon the always
already there with no
beginning and no end.

He saw how his
own beginning
and ending mirrored
eternity since as
a fetus and infant

he was buried in
time past and
time future
the envelope
of being in time.

When the immediate
views the unknown
of time past
and time future
the artist meditated
his way into
the living moment.

It is that the immediate
conceived itself
as a series of now points
and is grounded by
cosmic consciousness.

So, the artist
climbs into the here
and now as endless
possibility triggers
a journey of thought
into the beyond.

Suddenly, an image
of beauty, Truth
and love cascades
before him and they

point to a two
dimensional existence
with a portal to
the other side of thought.

Mirroring the way
the Truth and
the life, his image
forms the here
in now into
the beyond with
the rhythm
of the universe
driving pure music.

*

Traversing eons
at the speed
of thought, Olivia
from oblivion sought
the peace beyond
understanding
in the here in now.

As the elements
that comprise
time past, left her
with wounds
deep and festering
she astro-projected

herself through her
brain waves onto
the essence of
the rhythm
of the universe.

It was with
the light of one
dimensional existence
that she stretched
the envelope of time
when she connected
to the brain waves
of an old man who
sat beneath a white oak
tree, deep in meditation.

Connecting to his mind
she appeared in his
inner eye.

Dancing in a mist
of radiant colors
she revealed herself
as a woman of the earth.

Startled by her image
he wanted to share
his life with this
figure of beauty, Truth
and love.

In an instant they bonded.

As they orchestrated
themselves into a center
of being toward Truth
the old man thanked
The Unknown God
for granting him true love.

Then, in the actual
she walked into his life.

*

Although wounded
from battle
with his pain
intense, Eagle
Hawk struck to
the heart of being
there, and he was
proved victorious.

With razor precision
e attacked the will
to power with Truth
to power, and the demons
of the here in now
retreated into nothingness.

With a liberated
mind and being

of the substance
of being toward Truth
he re-established
life, liberty, and
the pursuit of happiness.

It was through
the workings
of The Spirit of Truth
that Eagle Hawk
returned pure music
to the land of the free
and the brave.

How awesome grew
the land of the free
and the brave, as
Eagle Hawk reaffirmed
the place of The Uknown
God into the lives
of the remnant of believers,

It was the presence
of the way, the Truth
and the life that brought
the peace beyond understanding.

Then, as the crystal
crow wrote onto
the hearts of humanity
a message of beauty

Truth, and love
the world marveled
at the strength
of ca land from
sea to shining sea.

Although the anthem
of hope came from
the beyond, it tendered
to the here in now with
precious treasures.

How freedom is
a precious treasure.

*

As a celebration
of the soul dances
into mind, the always
already there sings
beauty, truth, and love
into the will to be
and trumpets pyramid
life, liberty, and
the pursuit of happiness
from a vertical column
of time.

It is the orchestration
of space in time

into pure music
filling the immediate
with echoes of the beyond
and the drums of eternity
release the anthem of hope
into the heart
of things in themselves.

Then, the scarlet rose
the artist's muse, fills
the image of endless
possibility with what
matters, and the artist
colors times and a half
with the sweat of sacrifice.

Riding the rhythm
of the universe
through meditation
he rises onto forevermore.

Then, he jumps
on his muscle
and iron, and speeds
toward the light
of one-dimensional
existence, as his
will to be speaks
Truth to power.

Catching the beginning

of the wind, being in time
penetrates the mysteries
of life, and his muse
blankets him with
the meaning of things
in themselves.

How the muse loves the artist.

How the artist cherishes the muse.

Possessed with passion
for The Spirit of Truth
they pronounce their
sacrifice in a parabola
of time, enabling access
to the beyond that carries
their soul to joy
and wonder through the way
the Truth, and the life.

CHAPTER 4: reflecting the beyond

How longing for what
matters in a world
of madness, when beauty
Truth, and love are
buried in twisted rhetoric
the artist looks
to the old man for hope.

Meditating on the way
the Truth, and the life
they reach with the deep
touch to unwind
the mysteries of life
finding the way
the Truth, and the life.

As self passes
through times
and a half onto
the other side
of what is there

the artist feels
the anthem of
hope, and thought
turns to star dust
in a vast sea
of being in time.

Then, the artist
awakens to the love
of The Unknown God
the mystery of life.

So, the artist sees
a smile in the sky
as trumpets deliver
the moment onto
eternity, and his
heart feels
the reflection of
space in time
unfolding into
splendor.

It is through
meditation that
he connects with
endless possibility
as the scarlet
rose opens the door
to the everlasting.

Coloring words with
the anthem of hope
the old man takes
the artist into the source
of pure music
and the scarlet
rose dances desire
into his heart.

With visions
of eternity, he paints
beauty, Truth
and love as
the landscape
of what matters.

*

After hours
in The Hard Rock Café
Annabel Lee sat
with Eagle Hawk planning
the next move for
the underground.

The old man shuffled
in the bar room
from the garden
accompanied by
Olivia from oblivion
on his arm.

Together, they reached
an understanding
that what was
going on with
the principalities must
be replaced by
the language of the people
by the people
and for the people.

The will to power
and twisted rhetoric
had destroyed
the land of the free
and the brave.

Truth had been
buried beneath the debris
of double speak.

They selected peppermint
birdie, who was a senator
to run for the office
of presidency.

Special interests had
overtaken the language
with false representation
and they had corrupted
much of the people's thinking
with devious intent.

The language
of the underground
must be founded upon
beauty, Truth, and love.

How, special interests
had robbed a nation
of dignity turning
the citizens into
mindless cattle.

Once a land
of the free
and brave had
become a nation
of decadence.

How, godless a nation
had become through
the jabberwocky
of the elite.

*

Then, as she passed
through the unknown
the scarlet rose
unearth hidden
meaning, the subtext
of what is, and
the drift of being

in nothingness.

Shadows of chilling cold
surrounded her, as death
spoke to her heart.

Although frozen in
the moment, she sang
pure music in praise
of The Unknown God.

As she found
herself in a wilderness
of upheaval, her
inner eye looked
to the way, the Truth
and the life.

Then, she surfaced
in a two-dimensional
existence, as her mind
carried her into
the other side
of being there.

Looking back through
the looking glass
of what matters, she
held true to the message
of being toward Truth.

Realizing her journey

into the unknown
was predicated
upon the depth
of Truth, the scarlet
rose leaped into
the here in now.

So, she found the promise
of Truth extended
far and wide, and must
be encountered with courage.

So, she learned
to explore the beyond
rather than the unknown.

Although the unknown
tested her constitution
with virtual reality
the beyond strengthened
the muscle of being in time
with veritable reality.

How much better to dwell
in the actual where the divine
defines what matters.

*

Meditating his way
to the other side
of the madness

in the world, he
spoke Truth to power
and the barriers
of space in time
crumbled.

To wield the sword
that penetrates
twisted rhetoric, he
put to death
the empire of
double speak
and pure music
cleansed him
of unrighteousness.

It was the season
when demons attacked
his mind with foul
images, but he
looked through
The window of beauty
truth and love
as his defense.

How the madness
in the world batters
mind with pain.

Then, she comes
to his side

dancing with
the rhythm
of the universe.

Reaching into his
heart, she plants
the deep touch
of devotion
and he feels
the restoration
of his will to be.

As trumpets sound
awakening him
to the way, the Truth
and the life, pure
music follows him
through meditation.

Then, enlightened
through The spirit
of Truth, he buries
twisted rhetoric
beneath the debris
of a wasteland.

Then, she takes him
to the source of love
the house
of The Unknown
God, and he rejoices

with praises.

*

Where despots silence
the voices of freedom
and being in time
rots in prisons
of twisted rhetoric
Lady Liberty fights
for life, liberty, and
the pursuit of happiness.

Although tyrants
incarcerate the here
in now with double
speak, the anthem
of hope opens
channels to beauty
Truth, and love
gifts from The Unknown God.

It is corrupting what
is trustworthy meaning
of reality through
multiplicity of values
while only actuality
reflects the divine
into the presence
of the here in now.

It is that the actual
speaks Truth to power
as the will to be endures.

Through visions
the old man's
thought of what
matters surfaces
as the blood
of forevermore flows
like rapid rivers.

To look through
the looking glass
of the crystal
crow, he hears
the color of trumpets
announcing the end
of twisted rhetoric.

Then, despots
hide in shadows
of being in
nothingness, and
they drink their own
blood of contempt.

So, beauty, Truth
and love carry
pure music
into the remnant

the freedom fighters.

*

How vast the horizons
of time, as the soul
reaches into the heavens
and the will to be
celebrates the redemption
of time through the workings
brought from the presence
of the way, the Truth
and the life.

Released from prisons
of doubt, she looks
through the looking
glass of what matters
and visions of a house
of many mansions
radiates with beauty
Truth, and love.

As she dances
with the wind
she feels the glory
of The Unknown God
as mountains leap
into the sky.

It is that she

has found her soul
after living in doubt.

To grasp what matters
how the heart feels
life for the first time
as The Spirit of Truth
fills her with breath.

Although twisted
rhetoric burdened
her with boundless
doubts, she traveled
far beyond time past
as she entered life
liberty, and the pursuit
of happiness.

It was the feeling
of joy and wonder.

So, the old man knew
her as a true spirit.

So, he joined her
in the adventure
into endless
possibility.

Free from darkness
she lived with the light
of a vertical column

of time.

*

In shadows of being
in nothingness, when
time staggers with painful
thoughts, mind reflects
the always already there
of what matters.

Confined to a cell
the artist turns
to his faith
in The Unknown God
as he meditates
himself into the beyond.

There is no holding
back a free spirit.

Then, he recalls
The triumphant
return of pure
music, and he
looks through
the looking glass
of his will to be
finding relief.

While chained down
onto an iron bed

he navigates his
thoughts to images
of wonder.

Then, he feels pure
music surround
him with beauty
Truth, and love.

Although a prisoner
in the war of
principalities
his faith in
the way, the Truth
and the life liberates
him, as he images
a visitation of his muse.

She is lovely, and
he recalls her
deep touch.

Although he suffers
in solitary
confinement, the
moment reveals
the mysteries of life
through his desolation.

*

Although the realities

represent forms
of what is there
the actual defines
the Truth of being
in time.

While a prisoner
of double speak
in solitary
confinement
the artist reaches
into the deep
touch, and he
feeds on the manna
of his faith
in The Unknown God.

So, he reads
the writing on
the wall, grasping
the hidden meaning
of despots, and he
rejects the twisted
rhetoric of his
confinement.

Longing for times
of freedom, he finds
peace in the way
the Truth, and the life.

With his inner eye
he sees through
the looking glass of
the will to be, and
the artist leaps
into horizons far
beyond the here
in now.

In his mind, he
travels to the land
of the free and brave
as he listens to
the rain pounding
against a small window
in his cell.

It reminds him
of the splendor of
the drums of eternity
cascading through
the immediate
and leading the march
by Lady Liberty
across the globe.

To live and let live
rose in his heart
as his mind recalled
the embrace of the scarlet
rose, as his inner eye

foresaw the splendor
of her body dancing
through space in time.

*

Meditating on a stand
of trees, as light filters
through the leaves, forming
patterns on the earth, she
believes her way to beauty
truth and love.

How tall the trees
that touch the above
as she feels the rhythm
of the universe carry
her far into the beyond.

It is her faith
in The Unknown God
that gives her
a soul, something
previously unknown
to her.

A soul, to her
was a fiction
accepted by fools
until the old man
taught her the way

the Truth and the life
and The Spirit of
Truth opened her
to the deep touch.

Although an extra-terrestrial
she accepted that she too
had a soul.

So, she knew
that she had
a purpose, the purpose
to serve the Maker
of the heavens and earth.

It is love
that she feels for
the gift of a soul
and life exploded
with what matters.

So, she saw
the multitude
as children
of God, fashioned
in the image
of God almighty.

To live without
faith is to die
as a fool.

Then, she felt
the blessings
of life forevermore.

Then, she stood
before the stand
of trees as
a creature given
the grace of a soul.

*

Although despots try
to corrupt what is
there with twisted
rhetoric, the will to be
perseveres by
speaking Truth to power.

It is the will
to power disguised
as the desire
to serve that
despots dress
their language
with double speak.

As the despots
twist language
to suit their
purpose of control

they disarm
the populace
of weapons.

To numb the populace
until the people
surrender their freedom
the despots control
all aspects of life.

Thus, the populace
becomes slaves
living in the despair
of being in nothingness.

However, the children
of God arm themselves
with the power
and might from The Spirit
of Truth, arming themselves
to battle against
the tyranny forced
upon them through
the darkness of
double speak.

Those who control
the language, control
thought and behavior.

By speaking Truth

to power, the underground
battles the forces of evil.

It is the war
of principalities
in the land
of the free and brave.

How the freedom
fighters muster
the strength to
prove victorious
with the help of
The Unknown God.

*

Listening to pure
music as his trance
carries him onto
horizons hungry
for Truth, the artist
opens his inner eye
to the way, the Truth
and the life.

Thinking back
to the time
when he was
imprisoned
he saw how

injustice rules
with an iron fist.

There was a time
when he wondered
if God had
forgotten him
as the walls
of his cell
closed in on him.

Gaining his freedom
took a heavy price
although he remained
a wanted man.

It was an escape
from a cage that
brought him
into the end
of his incarceration.

Although he was
a hunted man
he found peace
through the mercy
of The Unknown God.

So, now he was
a fugitive
on the run

and he found
shelter in
The Hard Rock Café.

Joining the underground
he painted life
as a thought
carried by the wind.

So, he knew captivity
and he knew freedom.

How precious
he deemed freedom.

*

As pure music carried
thoughts far into
the beyond as
his brainwaves
followed the light
of vertical column of time
into vast surging seas
the artist climbed
out of himself
into what matters.

It was the triumph
over twisted rhetoric
that brought beauty
Truth and love as

the world celebrated
with the anthem of hope.

It was that the way
the Truth, and the life
delivered the peace
beyond understanding.

Then, the despots
of double speak
scattered into tangles
of despair, as pure
music released joy
and wonder.

As savage darkness
had ruled over
the heart of the world
with days and nights
of terror, the artist stood
his ground, and he painted
with the colors of life, liberty
and the pursuit of happiness.

Although twisted rhetoric
had crippled thought
the artist liberated
minds with the glory
of The Unknown God.

There was a portal

to the other side
of being in time
that took the madness
of the world
into the no longer.

Then, the artist
composed the meaning
of the deep touch
as pure music
encompassed
the living moment
and he found his time
redeemed by
The Spirit of Truth.

So, the scarlet rose
sang Truth across
all horizons of time.

*

Wrapped in the linen
of stars and stripes
and paraded through
the streets of forevermore
being toward Truth triumphed
over being there, a state
stagnant and centered
on preserving the will
to power.

There was the celebration
of souls across
the land as the breath
of the will to be found
the way, the Truth
and the life in what matters.

Chanting the anthem
of hope, the scarlet
rose silenced the demons
by reflecting the peace
beyond understanding.

As Lady Liberty danced
in the light of one
dimensional existence
Canis Lupis spoke
Truth to power
and the architect
of twisted rhetoric
joined the no longer.

While the drums
of eternity echoed
within hearts and minds
being in time was chosen
to follow the rhythm
of the universe into
the presence of the always
already there, the kingdom
of The Unknown God.

Looking to the crystal
crow, being toward Truth
heard the words
of Truth to power
collapse double speak
and despots scattered
into the domain
of being in nothingness
to dwell there forevermore.

Then, life, liberty
and the pursuit
of happiness became
the doctrine of
the landscape
and the children
of God sang pure music
across the globe.

How, endless times
rejoiced in the glory
of The Unknown God.

*

With visions of eternity
The Unknown God conceived
beauty, Truth, and love
as the elements of the will
to be, the seeds of being
in time, and an old man

pyramided into the peace
beyond understanding
through the way, the Truth
and the life.

As the body of pure
music passed into
the present, a figure
of darkness over
shadowed being in
time but the old
man dissolved
thoughts from
the dark side
from being there.

Then, he orchestrated
mysteries of life within
the center of things
in themselves.

It was The Spirit of Truth
that guided him to
the rhythm of the universe.

Wave upon wave
of thoughts shone
upon the need
in his heart
as his faith
in The Unknown
God grew into

the moment
of being toward
Truth.

As time present
exploded into the always
already there, the old
man caught a glimpse
of Olivia from oblivion
and she was the movement
of the elements of the will
to be from the mysteries of life.

Then, she erased
double speak
from linear reality
and enlightenment filled
the air with star dust.

Although darkness
overshadowed the moment
endless possibility
opened his inner eye
to the light of time
being redeemed
by The Unknown God.

*

In the calm
of a hot summer day
the mind explores

a garden where blossoms
punctuate the earth
with rare Truths.

It is that beauty
reflects what matters
as its life connects
to the divine.

Evoking thoughts
of all things meaningful
the garden speaks
to the heart
of the will to be
with its scent
of wonder.

Although the heat
of the day is
oppressive, the garden
liberates the mind
with pure music.

As the stretch
of the green lawn
blankets the landscape
visions of the other
side of space in time
flourish in the mind.

Then, Olivia from oblivion

fashions her love
for the old man
into a mindscape of wonder.

As a gentle breeze
stirs the moment, she
opens her inner eye
to endless possibility
as her legacy forms
the joy of generations
to come.

How massive
the architecture
of beauty, as it
builds monuments
of passion.

There is meaning
in the sway
of beauty, as
Olivia from oblivion
opens her heart
to the splendor
of what is there.

Joining her in
the garden, the old
man touches her
cheek with tenderness.

*

CHAPTER 5: thought beyond the immediate

Suddenly, the passion
for Truth, grips the world
and a dawn of a new
age creases the sky.

Written in the hearts
of the multitude
pure music liberates
minds from chains
of twisted rhetoric.

It is that minds
learn to dwell
in the physics
of beauty, Truth
and love.

It is the death
of double speak
that gives the times
life, liberty

and the pursuit
of happiness.

Then, Annabel Lee
dances across the sky
and Eagle Hawk
embraces the moment
looking through
a looking glass
of visions onto
forevermore.

As they expand time
into eternity, the world
rejoices with faith
in The Unknown God.

It was only
a dream passing
through the old
man's meditation
as he opened
a portal to
a parabola of time
and he witnessed
blood rain down
from the sky.

Then, trumpets
pyramided the presence
of Truth into a world

of madness ruled by
twisted rhetoric.

How the mind aches for Truth.

How the heart yearns for Truth.

How the will to be
lives on with the breath
of The Spirit of Truth.

*

When the ache
of being in
nothingness overwhelms
the immediate
and darkness enshrouds
the light of hope
the old man turns
to the way, the Truth
and the life for deliverance.

Seeing him in dire
straights, Olivia
from oblivion surrounds
him with comfort
kissing him on his cheek.

There is certain
madness to the moment
as twisted rhetoric

pounds a void
into his mind.

How he tries to end
the numbness
to his brain, as his
heart strains for life.

Although attacked
by demons bursting
into his being in time
his will to be continues.

Then, he feels
The Spirit of Truth
open his inner
eye to an orchestration
of pure music
and the old man
walks through a looking
glass of what matters.

As he hears
the drums of eternity
calling him to believe
his way through
his pain, he abides in
the loving strength
of The Unknown God.

Although lost

in the tangles
of the moment, he
climbs out of himself
to beauty, Truth
and love.

Blossoming his mind
onto witnessing cosmic
consciousness, hope writes
into his heart. and the old
man pyramids joy and wonder
into his living moment.

*

As space in time
retreats into darkness
and a chill penetrates
bones, the artist colors
the will to be with
the light of forevermore.

Riding the rhythm
of the universe
to the end
of what is, he
separates being
toward Truth
from being there
as the weeping
of a guitar reflects

the loss of self.

Riding with him
into his trajectory
through being in
nothingness,
the scarlet rose
takes him to another
side of what is there.

While at the edge
of madness
the scarlet rose
trumpets the artist
into an awakening
and his burden
is no longer upon him.

Then, the chill
of the no longer
warms in
the embrace
with The Spirit
of Truth.

Then, the darkness
of being there
retreats into
harmless shapes
of shadows.

Although darkness
blinded him for
a moment, the scarlet
rose brought him
the light of a vertical
column of time
through the way
the Truth, and the light.

Although the potency
of being in nothingness
seemed overpowering
his faith pulled
him into the peace
beyond understanding
with the deep touch
of his muse
the scarlet rose.

What awesome symmetry
their substance formed.

*

As The Unknown God
redeems time, mankind
finds hope in life.

It is the hope
of life onto eternity
a good life forevermore.

Although a model
of thought fashions
infinity as the ultimate
reality, eternity eclipses
reality since it has no
beginning and no ending
as the existence of actuality.

Infinity has a beginning
but no ending.

No one knows
where he or she
was before birth.

No one knows
where he or she
will be after death.

So, the old man
sat beneath
a white oak tree
thinking things
in themselves, as
he listened to the pure
music of the wind
rustling through
heavily leaved trees.

Then, the sun broke
through the clouds

and warmth
penetrated his body.

It was the green
of life that took
him far into
the beyond, as
rain drops on the grass
glistened like diamonds.

Hungry for meaning
the old man looked
to beauty, Truth
and love to uncover
the mysteries of life.

Opening his inner
eye, he saw
his purpose, as
pondering the elements
of being in time.

Then, he shared
his thoughts
with the artist.

Then, they both
laughed at their folly.

*

Tender is the moment

when two lives feel
the deep touch, and
the rub of love binds
flesh onto flesh
as the artist and his
muse, the scarlet rose
join their bodies
in true love.

As he colors
the moment
with pure music
she rises into
the breath
of epiphany
and tears of joy
heat times and a half.

It is when the immediate
extends beyond the here
in now that they
feel the embrace
of forevermore.

Gently in his arms
she rests with a smile
glowing in the light
of a vertical column
of time.

As they experience

the after glow
of their embrace
they ride
the rhythm
of the universe
to a new life.

As husband and wife
they overcome
the madness of
the world and
only remain
in their authentic
article of their time
in space.

It is that
their love comes
from their faith
in The Unknown God
as the sensation
of their deep touch
follows the elements
of beauty, Truth
and love.

So, a child is
conceived with
the passion
of what matters.

*

Ever closer to the edge
where space in time
intersects being
and nothingness
she slips into
the substance
of an abyss
and cosmic clocks
stop the immediate.

How meaning sifts
through the fingers
of what is there
sinking into the sands
of the no longer.

Unearthing times
and a half, she explodes
with thoughts of eternity
as wonder fills
the air with the mysteries
of life.

Connecting thought
to things in themselves
the way, the Truth
and the life
opens her inner
eye to being in time

awakening her to
the light from a vertical
column of time.

So, her biological clock
reflects the moment
when a trumpet
announces the presence
of The Spirit of Truth
and she catches
the elements of
being toward Truth.

It is that she
rides the rhythm
of the universe
to what matters
as her thunder
and iron follows
the road to everywhere.

Then, her passion
for life extends
into the unknown
and trumpets alert
her to the restarting
of the immediate.

It is her will
to be that does
not compromise

life, liberty
and the pursuit
of happiness
as she speaks
the language of cosmic
consciousness,

*

Dancing down on
the rhythm
of the universe
as what matters
penetrates the mind
and a forest of
freedom calls out to
the heart, she
topples twisted rhetoric
while she speaks
Truth to power.

It is the liberation
of thought from
the prison
of linear time
and an opening
to forevermore.

Then, she mounts
her thunder and iron
heading for the freedom

of the road, as the sun
sets in pools of darkness
and she reaches the land
of stardust.

Leaving behind
the dread of being
in nothingness, and
following the way
the Truth, and the life
she feels the joy
of being with The Spirit
of Truth, that showers
her with the deep touch.

Then, she takes
to the wind
dancing with
the freedom of life
liberty, and the pursuit
of happiness.

Filled with cosmic
consciousness, she rattles
the bones of being there
and conquers the will
to power.

How reading the mysteries
of life opens the way
to a vertical column of time

and the domain of
The Unknown God, the source
of beauty, Truth, and love.

*

Standing in the brink
of being in nothingness
he listened to the wind
speaking through the trees.

It was another
side of being
in time when he
carried dread deep
within his heart.

There were shadows
Of times past bringing regret.

Driven by darkness
posed by demons
he knew he had stepped
across the line and
onto a twisted life
but that was long ago.

How folly followed
his youth until one
day that was past
and of the no longer.

Now, as an old
man, he understood
the role of evil
and he wanted no
part of it in his life.

Casting aside wicked
ways, he redefined
himself as being
in search of Truth
when pure music
flowed through
the trees and
the desire to serve
a greater good
opened his heart
to the way, the Truth
and the life.

Leaving behind
the folly of his
youth, he walked
into the light
of vertical
column of time
into the mercy
of The Unknown
God, when The Spirit
of Truth filled him
with hopes
of his time redeemed.

*

Riding the rhythm
of the universe
to the other side
of the here and now
basking in the light
of one-dimensional
existence, she rose
beyond herself
into the divinity
of the actual.

It was the awakening
of her inner eye
to the way, the Truth
and the life, that
enabled her to take
her brain waves
into the beyond
and cultivating
her being in time
into a fortress
of power and strength.

Armed with the weapons
of beauty, Truth
and love, she lanced
twisted rhetoric, killing
double speak
and consuming

of the void of darkness.

Burning down the citadel
where being there had
plotted the destruction
of life, liberty
and the pursuit
of happiness, she
established pure music
as the language
of being toward Truth.

Then, she turned
to the old man
connecting him
to the anthem of hope.

It was a dance
through the looking
glass of what matters
as the moon broke
through the clouds
and the rains stopped.

No longer did reality
have meaning.

No longer twisted
rhetoric ruled the air.

So, she had learned
the language of the actual.

*

Burdened by times
when madness
in the world devours
sensibilities, he sits
at the edge of being
in nothingness
and thought scatters
across a wasteland.

As the sun sets
on dreams gone
by, he listens
to silence, the empty
void of being there.

It is the dread
brought by
merciless chaos
that smothers him.

How senseless fate
upon his heart.

So, the attacks
of September 11th
and October 7th
provoke thoughts
that dissolve
in bitter silence.

No words compensate
these assaults on humanity.

As the guardian
of language, he
measures the volume
of nothingness
and sees
the corruption
of what matters.

To alter language
with twisted
rhetoric rises
in the air
of humanity and
meaning becomes
meaningless.

Buried by the debris
that clogs mind
thought caves in
and bitter silence
punctuates times.

Dwelling in thoughts
of time before times
he recalls the grace
that embraced him
when pure music
showered him with

life, liberty
and the pursuit
of happiness.

Hope springs eternal.

*

Although a prisoner
of hate In dungeons
of despair, the artist
speaks Truth to
power, and rivers
of thought pour
pure music into
his life, keeping
him with good spirits.

It is the bitter taste
of incarceration that
takes the heart into
images of no longer
and mind suffers
in the darkness
of confinement.

As a free spirit
solitary confinement
cannot break the artist
his will to be will
never be fettered.

To be convicted
of a crime, he
did not do
how twisted rhetoric
rules rampantly
in courts of injustice.

It was a violation
of free speech
that was his crime
having painted
a political statement.

Because the principalities
ruled with a razors edge
the artist would
not be considered
innocent as he painted
life, liberty, and the pursuit
of happiness.

There was freedom to fight for.

After years in prison
he was released.

She kept his spirit
close to her heart.

 While in the deep
pit of brutality
he knew

his muse would
not forsake him.

Annabel Lee kept alive
his hopes and dreams
because they were one union
the while through meditation.

*

Surging forward
through the abys
as darkness blinds
the moment, she feels
her way to a parabola
of time, and hope
fuels her mind
with the will to be.

To be caged
in a labyrinth
of double speak
how her heart
pounds for freedom.

To desire beauty
Truth, and love
breaks the chains
of her captivity
as The Spirit
of Truth guides her

onto what matters.

Then, she opens
her life to the way
the Truth, and
the life, and she
sees the light
of The Unknown
God, the light
from a vertical
column of time.

It is that being there
is a stagnation
of thought, indulging
 in self pity
in its will to power.

So, there is
the will to be
as the source
of being in time.

Being in time
has the authentic
article with her
purpose as being
driven by her will
to serve.

However, being in

time can choose
the language
of twisted rhetoric
leading to being
there as the will
to power.

It is by seeing
through her inner
eye that she accepts
the gift of pure
music, the workings
of The Spirit of Truth.

Looking into the window
of space in time
she feels the here
and now as a presence
exuding the actuality
of being toward Truth.

It is a quiet time
when her soft voice
penetrates the living
moment, and the light
of a vertical column
of time opens her
inner eye to her destiny
in what matters.

How she wants

to be part
of what matters.
as her heart
reaches into
the substance of
the mystery of life

Called by The Spirit
of Truth, she fills
the air with the anthem
of hope, and the world
hears her voice carry
beauty, Truth, and life.

Then, the artist
configures space
into endless possibility
as he embraces
the scarlet rose.

They feel the deep
touch of the everlasting
in their moment together.

As they dance
with pure music
in their heart
their mind pyramids
into star dust
across the night sky.

How the madness
of the world disappears.

Gathering times
and a half, they
eradicate twisted
rhetoric from
the vocabulary
of the here
and now, as
their faith in
the Unknown God
breaks the strongholds
of the will to power.

*

Walking through he unknown
with his inner eye opened
to things in themselves
the artist took
to the wind with
thoughts of forevermore.

It was the immediate
in the here and now
that left him empty
while rivers of images
painted the unknown with
the light of a vertical
column of time.

Then, the mysteries of life
danced into his mind.

Then, endless
possibility filled
his thoughts
with the other
side of the unknown.

As time passed
in the hollow
of darkness
the artist listened
to pure music
and he smiled.

Mounting his iron
and thunder, he sped
onto the highway
to everywhere as
he left the immediate
for the rhythm
of the universe.

Launched beyond space
in time, he broke
through the barriers
of linear time eclipsing
the treasures that carry life
to its destiny.

It was on
the other side
of what was
there, that he
neared the dwelling
of his love, his muse
the scarlet rose.

Together, they danced
in rivers of moonlight
their faces lit with
a wondrous glow.

Together, they formed
a moment precious
in its design.

*

As leaves on wings
of autumn carry thoughts
into things in themselves
pure music feeds the moment
with crisp images
of eternity, and the heart
clings to what matters.

It is the song sung
in the moonlight
that travels far
beyond the here in now

as trumpets pyramid
Truth into the will to be.

Then, she lifts
dreams into what
is there, and time
slips forevermore
into the immediate.

How falling leaves
empty life into
the chilling winds
that rip across
the face
of being in time.

How the moon
shapes wonder
into the moment
as star dust speaks
to her soul.

How void the jabberwocky
of being there, as it grips
a lost breath.

Drifting across the sky
silhouettes of clouds
speak of a longing
for what matters
as the breath

of being in time
breaks the moment
with endless possibility.

Then, being there
dresses times and
a half with gibberish
and darkness consumes
what is there.

It is the falling
of the seasons
that liberates
the mind with
thoughts of being
toward Truth.

Although the moon
surrounds her
with the half-light
of twisted rhetoric
pure music fills
the air with hope.

*

Then, a spark
of life enlightens
the mind to the way
the Truth, and the life
as hope fills the will to be

with the way through
being in nothingness.

Then, the dread
of being there
recedes from the present
and a renewed purpose
to serve The Unknown
God surfaces.

So, there is twisted
rhetoric through demons
that wound the heart
and destroy the mind.

So, there is The Spirit
of Truth that brings
the promise of peace
beyond understanding.

How long the longing
for the breath of life
when what is there
is debilitating.

To give up the good
fight is to surrender
to the madness
of the world.

To harness the power
connecting the will to be

to The Unknown God
what strength
of a multitude far
beyond imagination
restores the living
moment to the soul.

As the light
of a vertical
column of time
opens the inner
eye to what
matters, The Spirit
of Truth breathes life
into the here and now.

Although the dread
of being in nothingness
flourishes, pure music
delivers a message
of beauty, Truth
and love, and the glory
of God almighty brings
life now and forevermore.

*

At the edge of thought
where the passion
for Truth carries
mind into pure music

ideas surface from endless
possibility, and trumpets
awaken images
of what matters.

It is that The Unknown
God redeems time
from abomination .

While Canis Lupis rides
to the ends of what is there
on his thunder and iron
eternity spreads its wings
upon the blowing wind.

How liberating the sound
of the engine of his passion
as his want exceeds time
present, and he travels
to the other side
of thought, searching
for the purpose to be.

Then, he finds his love
peppermint birdie
and he connects
the source of all
love to The Unknown
God.

As he serves his love

with understanding
he sees a purpose
as connecting
to what matters
through being toward
Truth.

His ride
upon the rhythm
of the universe
matters.

His love matters
and his connection
to the soured
of love matters.

Then, he feels
The Spirit of Truth
In a living moment
And his inner eye
Looks through a portal
To a song of pure music.

It is beauty, Truth
and love that
matter as he
thinks his way
through thought.

Then, the drums of eternity

give him breath onto
forevermore through the way
the Truth and the life.

*

As the madness
in the world confounds
the purpose of life, now
the American dream
sinks into an abys.

As twisted rhetoric rips
a nation apart, Truth
is lost in the struggles
between divisions.

Finding in the fog
of double speak
beauty, Truth and love
dissolve in nothingness
and time begs for mercy.

Then, pure music
awakens hope
as the artist breaks
into images
of thoughts of wonder.

So, the artist
orchestrates the will
to be into the divinity

of the always already
there, picturing
what matters.

It is serving beauty
Truth, and love
along with witnessing
to The Unknown God
that stirs hope into being
and the heart follows
the drums of eternity
onto the promises
of The Spirit of Truth.

Then, his muse
the scarlet rose
dances beneath
the full moon
and her shadow
follows her
onto forevermore.

Climbing out of self
he opens his heart
to his muse
and together they
shape endless
possibility onto
quiet dreams.

*

As pure music takes
the heart far
from calamity
and thunder rolls
through veins, how
being toward Truth
consumes the darkness
within being there with
the light of forevermore.

It is the source
Found in the beyond
That liberates self
From desolation
Thrust by the madness
In the world.

It is that thev will
to be, the seed of self
feeds on The Spirit
of Truth, and follows
the way, the Truth
and the life to deliverance
from being in nothingness.

Although a fire
Storm of twisted
rhetoric threatens
self with forests
ablaze, being
toward Truth endures.

Then, the artist
paints with the blood
of always already
there, and the actual
divines passage ont
life forevermore.

It is the freedom
from double speak
that fashions
hopes and dreams
sung into memory
and lived throughout
the threshold
of what matters.

How thoughts fill
the living moment
with intimidations
of The Unknown God
and mind awakens
to pure music.

Then, he constructs
a parabola of time.

Then, visions
of what matters
flood the moment
with wondrous dreams.

*

Years passed
into dust
and the wind
blew with rage
as the artist
configured the coming
and going of time.

It was the thunder
of times and a half
that took his breath
into a parade of Truth
and he severed his
ties to demons
of darkness.

Stepping into the light
from a vertical column
of time, he accepted
the gift from The Spirit
of Truth, as he followed
the way, the Truth
and the life onto
the everlasting.

Then, the drums
of eternity taught
him to march
into battle against

double speak and he
learned the armaments
of pure music, beauty
Truth, and love.

As the artist dug
himself out of despair
his muse sang him
into the mysteries
of life, and time stopped
at the edge
of the no longer.

It was in a parabola
of time that he portrayed
being in time
fulfilling dreams
of being toward Truth
and trumpets pyramided
the crystal crow
into his mind.

Thinking into the deep
touch of what matters
he believed himself
into the presence
of The Unknown God
and the scarlet rose
exploded the times
with splendorous wonder.

Then, he rode
pure music with
the rhythm
of the universe
onto a house
of many mansions.

*

Within the interstices
of mind where thought
touches ideas, the mystery
of life launches images
that matter, and the artist
defines beauty, Truth
and love to the living
moments onto space
in time.

As he witnesses
the presence
of The Unknown God
the world rejects
madness, issuing
the peace beyond
understanding through
the way, the Truth
and the life, none other
than Jesus the Christ
the only begotten son
of God almighty.

Marching into battle
in the war of principalities
the artist follows The Spirit
of Truth in victory
over twisted rhetoric.

Then, the artist takes
the light from a vertical
column of time
and colors the definition
of the actual as
the trumpeting of the divine.

Then, the scarlet rose
reaches into his heart
with the boundless passion
of the will to be and
the strength to endure.
.
It is beauty, Truth
and love for pure
music that carries
them onto victory
over their fate
achieving their destiny
as the power of celestial
clocks numbers time
and times and a half
onto forevermore.

It is the immortal

body of pure music
that triumphs over
the darkness
in double speak
bringing the light
of one dimensional
existence onto the here
in now.

So, the artist
and his muse
marry what matters
to civilization.

*

As an existential
threat of being
in nothingness emerges
from the always already
there, the will to be fights
for life, and being in time
builds thought upon mind.

It is the spark
of being toward Truth
that launches self
into endless possibility
and the language
of pure music teaches
the way, the Truth

and the life into
hungry minds.

From linear time
to vertical column
of time through
a parabola of time
the inner eye proceeds
into enlightenment
and thought leaps
out of darkness
onto what matters.

Then, the drums
of eternity pound
life into the living
moment.

Although being in
nothingness threatens
self with pains, the heart
endures through
the madness
of the world and times
and a half allow
being in time to purpose
itself toward Truth.

So, the artist reaches
through images of what
is there to the other

side of being there
and trumpets open
the moment
to the everlasting.

Orchestrating the elements
of what matters
beauty, Truth and love
he colors thought
with life, liberty
and the pursuit of happiness.

Overcoming the demons
of double speak, the artist
builds upon the actual
to realize the divine
in what matters.

*

Through the looking
glass of the crystal
crow, mind sees
things in themselves
and the power of thought
unearths hidden
from the unknown.

Although shadows
of twisted rhetoric
shroud being in time

with dread and despair
faith in the way
the Truth, and the life
pyramids the will to be
into a triumphant destiny.

It is the living moment
of meditation bathes
in pure music, and
The Spirit of Truth
fortifies self with the power
and glory of The Unknown
God.

Then, she climbs out
of herself and she becomes
being toward Truth.

As times and a half
pass into the no longer
she takes to the wind
feeling her way
into an epiphany
of hopes and dreams.

So, she has conquered
the darkness of double
speak with the drums
of eternity, and the language
born from beauty, Truth and love
feeds her with visions

of the house of many mansions.

Taking her thought
far into endless
possibility she undresses
the unknown with
the quick of her mind
as the muscle
of her will to be
pumps her life
into forevermore.

Defining the moment
with passion, she believes
herself into proximity
with the splendor
of what matters, the actuality
of the always already there
and the light of one
dimensional existence.

*

So, it was in The Hard
Rock Café that Eagle
Hawk was bartending late
one night that he heard
a calling in the wind
a movement of mystery
and he had the taste
of total collapse.

As a murmuring
 in
the thick of times
the calling brought
sadness to mind
and Eagle Hawk
looked into darkness
for the reason for despair.

Voided by dread
the sound consumed
the living moment
leaving behind
no trace of meaning
except the blood
from the immediate.

It was that Eagle
Hawk felt the depth
of the abys at the door
and the mellow tones
of a cello carried thoughts
of quiet desperation.

He was both there and not there.

Then, the calling burst
into a clashing
of thunder, and thoughts
brought rumbling of war.

Although the visitation
of an unearthly element
stirred in his heart
Eagle Hawk saw
the dance of infamy
through the looking
glass of being in
nothingness.

As the chill of desperate
delirium struck him
to his bones, his body
trembled, and his mind
drank the blood of grief.

Then, visions of the battle
field with the gore
of human mutilation
opened his mind to fallen
soldiers, while he lived on.

How the past raged
in wounds of memories
imbedded in his life.

*

A wondrous dream
awakening to the dawn
of what matters, how
the heart thirsts

for the way, the Truth
and the life.

As the day draws
The breath of forevermore
Trumpets celebrate
The presence of
The Unknown God
And he feels pure music
Flow into his mind.

To hear the anthem
of hope enables
the will to be
to flourish
as The Spirit
of Truth moves
the soul to faith.

Then, he actualizes
himself as being
toward Truth.

Then, it is time
to battle the demons
of double speak.

It is that
being in time
aligns his inner
eye with beauty

as his presence
draws light from
a vertical column
of time.

It is this light
that endows him
with the purpose
to advance the way
the Truth, and the life
into battle with demons.

How the deep touch
of pure music moves
across times and
a half as the war
of principalities rages.

Then, the forces
of being in nothingness
weep in despair
drifting in the no longer.

*

Before the unknown
the painted
dreams of the peace
beyond understanding
as the presence
of an existential

threat battered his mind.

As he bowed before
the way, the Truth
and the life, The Spirit
of Truth carried his
heart to the terrain
of beauty, Truth
and life eternal.

It was the shattering
of twisted rhetoric
that his mind mastered
the liberation
of his will to be
and thoughts pyramided
endless possibility
into a parabola of time.

Then, the artist
peeled away the shroud
of hidden meaning.

Then, the image
of what matters appeared
in colors of splendor.

As those colors filled
times and a half
the moment spoke
Truth to power

the demons
of double speak
trembled for their
end had come.

Although his faith
grew strong, he longed
for The Unknown God
to fill the world
with the presence
of being toward Truth.

Looking into the teeth
of twisted rhetoric, he
knocked out desperation
as he overcame
the demons within.

Then, the drums
of eternity pounded
life into the living
moment, and trumpets
break the silence of dread
with the anthem of hope.

*

Fighting against
the existential threat
born from double speak
the language of demons

and tyrants, all those
possessed by the will
to power, Lady Liberty
awoke a nation
to life liberty, and
the pursuit
of happiness
the right fist
of beauty, Truth, and love.

She waved the banner
of the way, the Truth
and the life, as she
stood before the world
as the anthem of hope.

There was strength
in the constitution
of her will to be
and grit in her gut
when she led an army
into the dwelling
of man's madness.

She held that The Spirit
of Truth must be
the doctrine of the landscape.

Then, Lady Liberty called
upon The Unknown God
to preserve the integrity

of the language, for if
language is corrupted
humanity would be lost.

Although twisted rhetoric
dominated the air
with darkness for times
and a half Lady Liberty
turned to the way, the Truth
and the life for the resurrection
of human integrity and dignity.

It was winning
the war of principalities
that restored beauty
Truth, and love
the elements of what matters.

So, Lady Liberty
brought the light
of freedom
to the darkness
of the desolate
through the blood
of The Lamb of God
Jesus the Christ.

*

In the garden
of The Hard Rock

Café peppermint birdie
listened to the wind
through the trees
as the sky blue
reflected eternity
and she saw a house
of many mansions
through her inner eye.

Although the sun
On her back
Warned her
The autumn air
Instilled a chill
To her bones.

With Canis Lupis
at her sided, as time
passed, the rhythm
of the universe
led them onto the always
already there and trumpets
pyramided life into
the living moment.

Then, she felt
the calling to serve
The Unknown God.

She spoke to him
what she felt and he

caressed her cheek.

He told her
her calling was
his calling and
he would be
at her side
no matter where
they were.

As they sat
listening to the anthem
of hope carried
by the wind, those chimes
of crystal bells
a door appeared open
and they entered
the chambers
of the president.

So, peppermint birdie
became Lady Liberty
and served with dignity
and strength in the land
of the free and brave.

So, Lady Liberty served
as president of United
States of America.

*

A melody of pure
music drifted
through space in time
as star dust waved
in the eve of
wondrous dreams.

As Truth endures
through the always
already there, the light
of a vertical column
of time destines Lady
Liberty to be the figure
head of freedom.

Following the drums
of eternity, she met
her destiny as the leader
of nations, but there
were those who
sought her death.

There are those
who hold the freedom
of the land of the free
and the brave as
a testament to evil.

With all the strength
of her conviction
to win the war

of principalities
she mobilized the allies
against the axis of evil
paralyzing the enemy.

So, they plotted her assassination.

It was her fate
that she died
In a plane crash.

The cause of the crash was hidden.

Then, the world spun out of control.

Weakened by the death
of their leader, the allies
floundered and the axis
of evil prevailed.

It was a dark time.

*

As a young boy
his father asked him
what matters.

He shrugged his shoulders.

His dad said
To pursue life, matters

to pursue beauty, Truth
and love matter
to go on a journey
whether in the mind
the world, or the universe
all matter.

What you do matters
and to pursues true love
matters.

Pure music matters along
with moments of silence.

Your family matters
and your friends, too.

It was times later
that he recalled
his dad's words

He had found
his life as a journey
into endless possibility
pursuing beauty, Truth
and love.

He found meaning
in the pure music
of a lover's kiss
in her deep touch
revealing the mysteries

of life.

He found the anthem
of hope. pounding
with every beat
of his heart.

How his memories
were filled with wonder
as he traveled
through space in time.

He found meaning
in his faith in
The Unknown God
in the way, the Truth
and the life, as well
as in The Spirit of Truth.

All this and more
he learned, matter.

*

There was a time
when pure music
died, and language
lost its meaning.

It was a dark time
and the heart
of humanity longed

for the return
of life, liberty
and the pursuit
of happiness.

Beauty, Truth
and love lived
in those of
the underground
and they readied
to bring back
freedom to the land
of milk and honey.

As the dark time
crumbled under
its own weight
of corruption
and as twisted
rhetoric staggered
beneath its hidden
meaning, the underground
struck down the bastions
of decadence.

As pure music stirred
the hearts of
the underground
the resurrection
of language led
the end of tyranny

that inflicted the land
of the free and brave.

It was the restoration
of beauty, Truth
and love as the doctrine
of the landscape.

It was a time
when peppermint
birdie rose as
a leader of promise
and she returned life
to the land.

So, the voice
of the people
spoke Truth
to power and
being toward Truth
flourished while
guided by The Spirit
of Truth
The Counselor
through all times.

*

As the soft music
of her voice echoes
in his heart, although

the prison walls close in
he remembers her
anthem of hope
and the walls dissolve.

The cries of his
fellow inmates awoke
him to the plight
in his desolation
as he longed
for freedom and
the times with
his true love.

Although confined
to a cold cell
his will to be
was strong as he
longed for his release.

He knew that
some day he
would taste
freedom again.

With no one to talk to he
survived with his memories
of her deep touch.

Then, one day came
when he was released

from his cell, and
released into freedom.

How, precious freedom.

Together with his love
the scarlet rose, he mended
his wounds from confinement
and entered a world on the mend,

The underground had
won the battle against
tyranny, and Lady
Liberty led the world
into peace and prosperity.

Returning to his art
his paintings grew
more powerful.

There were colors
of hope, as pure
music embraced
true love, although
somber shadows edged
into his parabola of time.

*

So, the existential threat
of tyranny pursued being
in time as trepidations

stirred across the underground
and the heat of the pursuit
dominated with their will to power.

It was the attack
on the will to be
by twisted rhetoric
that corrupted minds
and turned the people
into mindless cattle.

A remnant remained faithful
to The Unknown God
as the underground
and The Spirit of Truth
remained with them.

How they persevered
through persecution
as the tight fist
of tyrants pounded
them at every turn.

Calling a local group
together at the Hard Rock Café
peppermint birdie established
an underground radio station.

They spread beauty
Truth and love
to a dark world.

Following the way
the Truth and the life
their will to be spread
the anthem of hope
across a nation.

It took a while
but they conquered
A tyrannical regime.

To speak Truth
to power wins out
although it takes
perseverance
and dedication.

To follow The Spirit
of Truth enables
being toward Truth
to meet any adversity.

Although the existential
threat dominated the doctrine
of the landscape, the underground
radio station brought sense to life.

CHAPTER 6: another day underground

It was a time
when purse music
set the air with
jewels of promise
and she kept
the flowers of her
heart in eternal
blossoming.

It was the dance
of dreams across
the living moment
that brought beauty
Truth, and love
into the terrain
of her mindscape.

As she looked
into the looking glass
of time in space
visions of splendor

rocketed the skies
and the scent of love
drank in tears of joy.

It was times and
a half later that she
felt the blunt
thrust of twisted
rhetoric pound her
poisonous thoughts
cloaked in darkness.

Then, a chill
fell across her heart
heaving noise into
her veins and she
wept her desolation
into rivers of spent blood.

As ghosts bearing
turmoil swept across
her consciousness
she fought against
the source of her
troubles, double speak
that corrupted language.

Although moments
of duress
shattered her mind
she overcame them

with the power
from meditating on
the way, the Truth
and the life.

So, the will to be
endures trying times
upon listening to
The Spirit of Truth.

*

A wondrous dream
awakening to the dawn
of what matters, how
hungry the heart
for the way, the Truth
 and the life.

As the day draws
the breath of forevermore
trumpets celebrate
the presence of
The Unknown God
across times and a half
and he feels the force
of pure music in his mind.

To hear the anthem
of hope allows
the will to be

to flourish
in moments
as The Spirit
of Truth speaks
to the soul.

Then, he actualizes
himself as being
toward Truth.

Then, it is time
to battle the demons
of double speak.

It is that
being in time
aligns his inner
eye with beauty
Truth and love
as his presence
draws from the light
of a one dimensional
existence.

It is from this light
that endows him
with the purpose
to advance the way
the Truth, and the life
into battle with
the demons.

How the deep touch
of pure music
moves across times
and a half into the war
of principalities.

Then the eyes
of being in
nothingness
weep in the despair
of drifting in the
no longer

*

Before the unknown
the artist painted
dreams of the peace
beyond understanding
as an existential threat
battered his mind.

As he bowed before
the way, the Truth
and the life, The Spirit
of Truth carried his
heart to the terrain
of beauty, Truth and love.

It was the shattering
of twisted rhetoric

that his muse modeled
the liberation of his
will to be, and thoughts
pyramided endless
possibility into a parabola
of time.

Then, the artist
peeled away the shroud
of hidden meaning.

Then the image of
what matters appeared
in colors of wonder.

As those colors filled
times and a half
the moment spoke
Truth to power, and
the demons of double
speak trembled for
their end had come.

Although his faith
was strong, he longed
for The Unknown God
to fill the world
with the presence
of being toward Truth.

Looking into the jaws

of twisted rhetoric
he knocked out
desperation, as he
overcame the darkness
within.

Then, the drums
of eternity marched
life into the living
moment, and trumpets
broke the silence
of dread with
the anthem of hope.

Then, the artist smiled.

*

Fighting against
the existential threat
of double speak
the language of demons
and tyrants, all those
possessed by the will
to power, Lady Liberty
founded a nation
upon life, liberty
and the pursuit
of happiness, the tight
fist of beauty, Truth
and love.

She waved the banner
of the way, the Truth
and the life, as she
stood before the world
as the anthem of hope.

There was strength
in the constitution
of her will to be
and grit in her gut
when she led an army
into the dwelling
of man's madness.

She held that The Spirit
of Truth must be the doctrine
of the landscape.

Then, Lady Liberty called
upon The Unknown God
to preserve the integrity
of the language, for if
language is corrupted
humanity would be lost.

Although twisted rhetoric
dominated the air
with darkness
for times and a half
Lady Liberty turned

to the way, the Truth
and the life for
the resurrection of human
dignity and integrity.

It was winning
the war of principalities
that restored beauty
Truth and love
the elements
of what matters.

So, Lady Liberty
brought the light
of freedom
to the darkness
of a desolate world.

*

In the garden
of The Hard Rock Café
peppermint birdie
listened to the wind
through the trees
as a sky of blue
reflected eternity
and she saw a house
of many mansions
through her inner eye.

Although the sun
on her back
was warm
the autumn air
instilled a chill
into her bones.

There ws Canis Lupis
at her side, as time
passed with the rhythm
of the universe
leading her onto the always
already there, and trumpets
pyramided life into
the living moment.

Then, she heard
the call to serve
The Unknown God.

Then, she spoke to him
what she felt, and he
caressed her cheek.

He told her that
her calling was
his calling, and
he would be
at her side
no matter where
she went.

As they sat
listening to
the anthem
of hope carried
by the wind, those
chimes of crystal
bells, a door appeared
open, and they entered
the oval office.

So, Lady Liberty
became president
of the land of
the free and brave.

*

A melody of pure
music drifted
through space in time
as stardust waved
in the dawn
of what matters.

As Truth endures
through the always
already there, the light
of a vertical column
of time destined
Lady Liberty to be
the figure head

of freedom.

Following the drums
of eternity, she met
her destiny as the leader
of nations, but there
were those who
sought her death.

There care those
who hold freedom
in the land of the free
and brave as
a testament to evil.

They held their own
brand of beauty, Truth
and love through
the will to power
and self-validation

With the strength
of her conviction to win
the war of principalities
she mobilized the allies
against the axis of evil
paralyzing them.

So, they plotted her assassination.

It was her fate
that she perished

in a crash
of Air Force One.

The government hid
the cause of the crash.

Then the world
spun out of control.

Weakened by the death
of their leader, the Allies
floundered, and
the Axis of evil prevailed.

It was dark times.

*

As a young boy
his father asked
him what matters.

He shrugged his shoulders.

His father proceeded
with a lesson from his heart.

he said to pursue life matters
to pursue beauty, Truth
and love matters
to go on a journey
whether in the mind

the world or the universe
all matter.

What you do, matters
and to pursue true love
matters.

Oure music matters along
with moments of silence.

Your family matters
 and your friends, too.

It was a time later
that he recalled
his dad's words.

He had found
his life as a journey
into endless possibility
pursuing beauty, Truth
and love.

He found meaning
in the pure music
of a lover's kiss
in her deep touch
revealing the mysteries
of life.

He found the anthem
of hope singing

into his heart and mind.

How wonder filled
his memories
as he traveled
through space in time.

He found meaning
in his faith in
The Unknown God
the way the Truth
and the life, as well
as The Spirit of Truth.

He had no need for self-validation.

He accepted who he was
as being toward Truth.

*

There was a time
when pure music
died and language
lost its meaning.

It was a dark
time and the heart
of humanity longed
for the return
of life, liberty
and the pursuit

of happiness.

Beauty, Truth
and love lived
in those of
the underground
and they readied
to bring back
freedom.

As dark times
crumbled under
its weight of corruption
as twisted rhetoric drowned
beneath its hidden
meaning, the underground
struck down the bastions
of decadence.

As pure music stirred
the hearts of
the underground
the resurrection
of language led
the end of tyranny
that inflicted the world.

It was the restoration
of beauty, Truth
and love as the doctrine
of the landscape.

It was a time
when peppermint
birdie rose as
a prominent leader
and she gave life
to all lands.

So, the voice
of the people
spoke Truth
to power and
the will to be
flourished while
guided by The Spirit
of Truth, The Counselor
through all times.

*

As the soft music
of her voice echoes
in his heart, although
the prison walls close in
he remembers her
anthem of hope
and the walls go away.

The cries of his
fellow inmates awoke
him to the plight
of his destitution

and he longed
for freedom and
the times with his
true love.

Although confined
in a cold cell
his will to be
grew stronger
as he longed
for his release.

He knew some
day he would
taste freedom
again.

With no one to talk to
he survived with his
memories of her
deep touch.

Then, one day
after a long time
they released him
from his cell, released
him into a free world.

How, precious freedom.

Together, with his love
the scarlet rose, he mended

his wounds from prison
entering a world on the mend.

The underground had
won the battle against
tyranny, and Lady
Liberty led the world
into peace and prosperity.

Returning to his art
his painting grew
in Truth to power.

There were colors
of hope as pure
music poured the embrace
of forevermore, although
somber shadows weighed
into his parabola of time.

*

So, the existential threat
of tyranny pursued being
in time, as trepidations
stormed across the underground
and the heat of their pursuit
by the will to power dominated
dangerous times.

Attacking being toward Truth
twisted rhetoric corrupted

thoughts and turned the people
into mindless cattle.

A remnant remained
faithful to The Unknown
God as the underground
and The Spirit of Truth
guided them.

How, they persevered
through their struggle
as the iron fist
of tyranny pounded
them at every turn.

Gathering a local group
together in the garden
of Hard Rock Café
peppermint birdie
established an underground
radio station, speaking Truth
to power.

They spread beauty Truth
and love in a dark world.

Following the way
the Truth and the life
their being toward Truth
spread the anthem of
hope across the globe.

It took a while
but they conquered
tyrannical regimes.

To speak Truth to power
proves victorious, although
it takes perseverance
and dedication.

To follow The Spirit
of Truth enables
being toward Truth
to face any adversity
head on.

Although the existential
threat dominated the doctrine
of the landscape, the underground
radio station brought sense to life.

*

As pure music filled
his mind with feathers
of splendor, and the scent
from her deep touch
pulled the artist into wonder
he stepped out of himself
into the light of vertical
of time.

There was majesty

in the sky, as his
thoughts traversed
the here in now
far into the beyond.

Then, the crystal crow
showed him beauty
Truth, and love found
in The Unknown God
and he wept at the sight
of eternal peace.

How, visions of
bliss forevermore
pyramided his mind
into images that
transcended space
lin time, and he
reached what matters
through the way
the Truth, and the life.

As images soared over
being in nothingness
he touched the heart
of pure music, beauteous.

Although ravenous
as an image, where
a certain desolation
resounded, it did not

overpower The Spirit
of Truth in his life.

As pure music
poured upon the canvas
the breath of the always
already moved mountains
into the clear sky.

Then, he felt the heart
of the crystal crow
pound his destiny
into the trumpeting
of what matters.

Gazing into the blue
of a looking glass
that opened a view
to a house of many
mansions, the artist
gave humanity a
wondrous meaning.

*

Although the existential
threat of twisted rhetoric
dominates the air
corrupting the language
being toward Truth
perseveres with a strong

faith in The Unknown God.

As double speak thunders
across times and a half
the will to be feeds
upon The Spirit of Truth.

So, the underground
gathered at The Hard Rock
Cafes across the globe
supporting their radio
free stations but tyrannical
regimes hunted them down.

It was that being in time
chose to fight for freedom.

There was blood in the streets.

Leading the resistance
Canis Lupis teamed
with peppermint birdie
who became known
as Lady Liberty.

Although tyrannical
regimes relentlessly
pursued the radio stations
the underground
protected them.

To live with a price

on their heads, how
life went to the quick
and the brave.

Escaping capture
they hid in the belly
of the earth.

So, at best life was difficult.

Wearing thin they
learned the meaning
of being in nothingness.

Hunted as criminals
how they struggled.

Although the pursuit
was great, they proved
victorious over
tyrannical regimes
and lands lived
in freedom.

*

As time wore
a stony path
through heart
and thoughts ebbed
into nothingness
the will to be

faced the will
to power, determined
to score a victory
over tyranny.

As being in time
struggled against
twisted rhetoric
visions of eternity
opened her soul
to The Spirit of Truth
and trumpets of what
matters showered pure
music upon her mind.

There was the flight
of golden leaves
across the sky
and she felt
the embrace
of the always
already there.

As the crisp air
creased her living
moment she looked
to the crystal crow,

Then, the drums
of eternity took
her dreams to

the other side
of times and
a half where
pure music
consumed
double speak.

Knowing victory
over tyrannical
regimes neared
she sang an anthem
of hope into
the darkness of being
in nothingness.

It was a time when faith
in The Unknown God
delivered a people
to a promised land.

Then, the crystal
crow led the people
into bastions
of twisted rhetoric
and freedom reigned
across the globe.

*

During the ticking
of the biological

clock, self journeys
through the unknown
and the madness
of the world is there.

How, the heart
searches for beauty
Truth, and love
as the will to be
probes endless
possibility, and
being in time hears
the call of The Spirit
of Truth.

Then, being toward Truth
endowed with the promise
of the way, the Truth, and
the life, serves The Unknown
God with devotion.

In him was
the substance
of life, the elements
that matter, and
victory over
twisted rhetoric.

Although she thought
herself destitute
in the no longer

she prayed for deliverance
and found it
in the brain waves
sent through the old man's
meditations.

Turning into his
emanations
she came to his
side after times
of searching
the universe
for true love.

It was that his
brainwaves were
attuned to
the rhythm of
the universe, and
transcended space
in time.

*

CHAPTER 7: vitally into the deep touch

Awakening to trumpets
of glory, when the dawn
of the everlasting stretched
across all horizons, she
journeyed to the other
side of despair, drinking
in the left over time.

As she sat at the edge
of being in nothingness
she heard the calling
of The Spirit of Truth
and times shifted to
moments with pure music.

There was the rhythm
of the universe gathering
in the corners of her
mind, as she meditated
herself beyond space
in time.

Orchestrating the colors
of times and a half
she met her fate
in shades of blue
covering the sky with
a vision of her destiny.

Then, the dawn
of what matters
moved her heart into
hopes and dreams.

So, echoes of the drums
of eternity carried
her far beyond the madness
in the world, and she
opened her inner eye to
horizons of splendor.

Leaving behind the dreary
barriers of linear time
she eclipsed the here
in now with intimations
of the beyond
and passion filled
her veins with purpose.

To serve The Unknown
God with the devotion
for life forevermore
she mounted her

destiny, traveling
with the way, the Truth
and the life, as time
shifted to the minute
particular.

It was a moment
when times
entered the pure
music of true love
and she felt
the approach of
the light of one
dimensional existence.

*

There is a song
in the wind that
carries Truth
to those traveling
through the unknown.

Upon hearing
pure music awaken
the mind to what
matters, the soul rises
from the debris
left by the madness
in the world.

How riders upon
the rhythm
of the universe
carry the anthem
of hope in
their heart, and
the sky opens
to the dawn
of forevermore.

As their faith feeds
upon The Spirit
of Truth, their will
to be pounds
twisted rhetoric
into dust.

As being in time
chooses the way
the Truth, and
the life, being toward
Truth emerges
and trumpets
celebrate the coming
of beauty, Truth
and love upon
this earth.

Longing for life
liberty, and
the pursuit

of happiness
those who dream
for freedom
from double
speak wave the flag
of stars and stripes.

Although the wind
teaches language to
think beyond the moon
and stars, linear
time rejects
hopes and dreams
but the will to be
fights a fate
of destitution
and the drums
of eternity pound
a destiny of Truth.

After the end
when space
in time eclipsed
being there, Annabel
Lee celebrated
the moment by
meditating upon
The Spirit of Truth
and the world
of madness fell
into the no longer.

As she sang
pure music across
the air, clouds
rained blossoms
of wondrous
delight, and she
swept away all
twisted rhetoric
from the globe.

It was a time
when the light
of one-dimensional
existence pulled
her into an epiphany.

Then, she fed
the will to be
with mana
from heaven.

Then, she opened
her inner eye
to an age
when life, liberty
and the pursuit
of happiness became
the doctrine
of the landscape.

After she danced

freedom into the living
moment, Annabel
Lee drank in images
belonging to the other
side of the no longer
and her mind climbed
into the beyond.

There was a trumpeting
of time and times
and a half as she
rode the rhythm
of the universe
into pure music
and the scent
of beauty, Truth and love
enfolded her body
with a sweet fragrance.

So, it was the end
finally
of double speak.

*

As a voiced that
changed the world
where double speak
broke minds with
twisted rhetoric
the voice of The Spirit

of Truth moved
hearts into eclipsing
space in time
and a herd of pigs
drowned in a river.

It is the herd
that follows
false prophets
into ignominy
and the wrath
of eternal death
in a lake of fire
fills them with
 angst forevermore.

How in the shallows
where double speak
massages minds
with twisted rhetoric
thoughts cave into
the banal, and Truth
writhes riddled with
meaninglessness.

As the world turns
wrong and silence
bleeds Truth into
the vacuous
how the heart
yearns for what

matters.

When beauty Truth
and love are tarnished
by minds cast
into the void, how
sadness fills the heart
of the artist, and he
opens his mind to
pure music where hope
is eternal, and thoughts
unearth hidden meaning.

Then, the muse rubs
him with pure music.

So, there is hope
for him and mankind
by rejecting the madness
of the world, and believing
in The Unknown God.

*

As pure music fills
him with what matters
and the last trumpet
breaks across the horizon
mind travels to the other
side of being in nothingness.

As thunder roars

through his veins
and the heat
of the times
bakes his brain
he recalls her voice
carrying beauty
Truth, and love.

Although the rhythm
of the universe brings
her lips to a kiss
it is a dream gathered
in the wind.

Them, the dream
reaches the embrace
of the deep touch
and he looks
to the moon dancing
silently across the sky
for true love.

It is a time of memories.

It is the sweet
scent of her
wonder crossing
over the moment
that he bleeds
a bottle dry.

Drunk again on
times in a half
he rockets into dreams
and his life turns
into star dust.

Then, times later
her death gave
him the Truth
of his true love.

Alone, he wandered
through alleys of darkness.

As time, and times
and a half passed
he found himself
at the beginning
of life, liberty
and the pursuit
of happiness.

Finally, Canis Lupis
was free from grief.

*

Possessing the authentic
article brought her
soul to the way, the Truth
and the life, as the breath
of The Spirit of Truth filled

her with the passion
to serve The Unknown God.

As a grain
of sand yielded
eternity in the hour
glass of the crystal
crow, she walked
through a furnace
confining her
in the madness
of the world
while she held her
faith close to her heart.

although flames
consumed times
and a half, she
carried onjto
another time
present through
meditation upon
the glory of
The Unknown God.

It was her destiny
As she rode the rhythm
Of the universe to believe
In God almighty.

As a rebel

Olivia from
oblivion took
to the sky
following brain
waves through
eternity until
she found a place
in the heart
of an old man.

Then, pure music
flowed through
her mind and she
took the form
of his sweetheart.

Together, they traveled
across a parabola of time
to a house of many
mansions, while they
stayed inside eternity
but in the here and now
they kept their promise
of true love.

Together, they defined
true love in the blood
of what matters.

*

As star dust in the wind
the children of God
carried the message
of the way, the Truth
and the life, sharing
with the world
The Spirit of Truth.

They were true
and they were
faithful to
The Unknown God
as they faced
the darkness
of a dark world.

Rejecting them
abusing them
and torturing them
the world only
thirsted for their blood
yet, the children
of God persisted.

After times and
a half, parts
of the world listened
to their message
and followed
the way, the Truth
and the life

onto forevermore.

Then, the world
collapsed and
tyrants ruled.

Then a great
persecution
of the faithful
followed, until
only a remnant
remained.

They became the underground.

Living in shadows
hiding beneath rocks
they scurried
from one place
to another.

Peppermint birdie
proved a fierce
leader
of the underground
accompanied
by Canis Lupis.

Together, they spoke
Truth to power
across the airwaves
growing a force

that one day
toppled the tyrants.

*

The blood of the age
streamed to the seas
and the fury of godless
tyrants brought ruin.

As darkness consumed
the minds of the world
a cry for freedom
brought the light of hope.

Across the land
Radio Free America
spoke Truth to power
and the people listened
with thirsty minds.

Armed with the way
the Truth, and the life
they stormed the bastions
of decadence, ridding
the land of double speak.

Peppermint birdie
leading the cause
of life, liberty, and
the pursuit of happiness
took faith in The Unknown

God into the battlefield
and flames devoured
the tyrants.

It was not
a time to turn
the other cheek.

It was time
to take a stand
against oppression
and restore freedom
to the land.

It is through freedom
that the faithful could
worship The Unknown God
openly, and teach their
children what matters.

So, The Spirit of Truth
filled the world with
the peace beyond
understanding.

As beauty, Truth
and love returned
as the doctrine
of the landscape
the anthem of hope
filled the world

with pure music.

*

Meditating his way
to beauty, Truth, and love
the old man communed
with The Spirit of Truth
and a portal to the beyond
opened a vertical column
of time.

It was his biological
connected through
the celestial clocks
to the cosmic clock.

Then, he experienced
Truth preceding existence.

Then, meaninglessness
disappeared in times and a half.

Then, The Unknown God
Wrote a testament into
His heart, and life flourished
In meaningfulness.

Riding bthe rhythm
of the universe
the old man climbed
our of himself, and

his consciousness eclipsed
being in nothingness.

How the bastions
of twisted rhetoric
pounded being there
into minds, as humanity
fell into being cattle.

Then, being toward Truth
advanced across
the terrain, and thunder
roared with passion
in enlightened minds.

Then, pure music anointed
what matters as Truth.

Then, to serve
The Unknown God
purposed life
into the living moment.

As the breath
of The Spirit of Truth
carried the old man
into the always already
there, he reached
the deep touch.

So, his will to be
the seed of self

endures onto
forevermore.

*

Coloring the sky
with stardust
the artist configured
space in time, and
his muse danced
beneath a full moon.

As a parabola
of time pictured
eternity in a grain
of sand, the artist
fed a river of tears
to the ocean
and wave upon wave
of painful cries
echoed in minds
of political prisoners.

There were times
when he sunk
in swamps, where
his heart dwelt
in desperation
but those times
became memories
visiting him in shadows.

He learned how pure
music buried the cries
of times past.

He learned how
meditating upon
The Unknown God
helped remove
his pain.

He learned how
The Spirit of Truth
healed the tormented
mind as he believed
in deliverance from
the way, the Truth
and the life.

The image driven
by beauty, Truth
and love broke
the chaos that loomed
so long across the world.

As the anthem
of hope comforted
hearts, twisted
rhetoric no longer
found a place
in humanity.

Then, the artist
depicted a dawn
over evening's twilight
as stormy clouds
passed into distant
horizons.

*

 As the eve
of destruction
broke across
the horizon
and space
in time
collided with
chaos, Olivia
from oblivion
took her will
to be into
a parabola
of time.

Traveling far beyond
Any here and now, she
Searched the universes
For a kindred spirit.

Sensing brain
waves, she tuned
into the meditation

of a man, distant.

Arriving at his sided
she found an old
man meditating
beneath a white
oak tree.

His face hung silent
As his body swayed
To the rhythm
Of the universe.

Feeling the sensation
Of a sudden warmth
He opened his eyes c
To a mature beauty.

Taking the form
of a beautiful
woman in her
fifties, she sat
at his side,

They smiled.

Then, the old
man played
a melody
of pure music
on his guitar
wooing her.

As she opened
his heart with
tender looks
he felt
the mysteries
of life stir
in his bones.

From then on
they were two
true spirits
destined to
forevermore
together.

*

Visiting alternate
realities in dreams
of what could be
lines of terror
fixed the eyes
onto hidden
meaning found
in the mysteries
of life.

As the fury
of endless
possibility inflamed
the heart with

a driving passion
for what was
there, the artist
portrayed
the colors
of eternity
in the blood
of the Lamb
Jesus Christ
The only begotten
Son of God almighty.

Then, a study
of the way, the Truth
and the life bled
being toward Truth
and trumpets awakened
the living moment
to beauty, Truth
and love.

As the artist opened
his heart to The Spirit
of Truth, reality
after reality revealed
hidden meaning
and his mind walked
to the other side
of space in time.

There was the immaculate

reign of what matters.

There was the echo
of pure music
in the mind
of his will to be.

As his muse
the scarlet rose
danced mysteries
into his bones
the artist saw
the drift of true
love in his life.

Then, alternate
realities encompassed
times and a half
And they took
the artist into
the light of
a vertical column
of time.

*